Automobile Business: A Guide: Helpful, Inspirational, And Suggestive

Jacob Harmon Newmark

Nabu Public Domain Reprints:

You are holding a reproduction of an original work published before 1923 that is in the public domain in the United States of America, and possibly other countries. You may freely copy and distribute this work as no entity (individual or corporate) has a copyright on the body of the work. This book may contain prior copyright references, and library stamps (as most of these works were scanned from library copies). These have been scanned and retained as part of the historical artifact.

This book may have occasional imperfections such as missing or blurred pages, poor pictures, errant marks, etc. that were either part of the original artifact, or were introduced by the scanning process. We believe this work is culturally important, and despite the imperfections, have elected to bring it back into print as part of our continuing commitment to the preservation of printed works worldwide. We appreciate your understanding of the imperfections in the preservation process, and hope you enjoy this valuable book.

RETURN TO
LIBRARY
67

Automobile Business

A Guide:

Helpful, Inspirational, and Suggestive

By

Jacob H. Newmark

Automobile Publishing Company
Detroit, Michigan

Transportation
Library

TL
154
.N56.

Copyright, 1915
BY
JACOB H. NEWMARK

PUBLISHED BY
AUTOMOBILE PUBLISHING COMPANY
DETROIT, MICHIGAN

INTRODUCTION

This book is for those who are already engaged in the automobile business, or who are thinking of entering this field of activity in any capacity, either as a dealer, salesman, in garage work, or the business as a whole.

It is a money-making business for those who do business according to the standards of the day; it is not money-making for those who are not methodical, businesslike, aggressive, energetic; who believe in waiting for business to come to them.

This book points out the money-making way.

It is offered with the hope that it will help those who are already in the business.

And that it will materially assist those who contemplate entering into it.

It is intended as a guide: helpful, inspirational, and suggestive.

JACOB H. NEWMARK.

CONTENTS

CHAPTER	PAGE
I.—Opportunities	1
II.—Choice of Territory	11
III.—Organization	15
IV.—Selection of Cars	23
V.—Show Room—Location—Windows	30
VI.—Salesmen	41
VII.—Salesmanship and the Prospect	46
VIII.—Car Knowledge	71
IX.—Advertising	84
X.—Promotion Work	93
XI.—Prices	97
XII.—Demonstrations	99
XIII.—Garage	105
XIV.—Service	109
XV.—Garage and Accessories	120
XVI.—Garage and Repairs	134
XVII.—Second Hand Cars	155
XVIII.—The Commercial Car	159
XIX.—Electric Vehicles	168

Contents

CHAPTER	PAGE
XX.—THE CAR AND THE WOMAN	175
XXI.—THE BOY OF TO-DAY	178
XXII.—YOU AND YOUR OPPORTUNITIES	180
XXIII.—PLAN AND THINK	184
XXIV.—TO-DAY IS THE DAY	191
XXV.—DON'TS	196

Automobile Business

CHAPTER I

OPPORTUNITIES

A good many years ago, a famous preacher addressed a gathering of six hundred boys. He spoke to them of their future and among other things, said: "Boys, you can be just what you want to be in this world. You can become a great merchant. You can become a successful doctor, or a lawyer. You can accomplish anything you set out to accomplish, but you will have to pay the penalty.

"And the penalty is work, concentration, and application."

And this rule applies with equal truth to all

men and to any business, including the automobile business.

Our success in this world is in proportion to our desire to attain it.

Today, business success is a question of effort.

Effort is produced by energy and the amount of energy we actually put in our work is governed by the strength of will power.

We receive just what we give—no more—no less.

It is the law of life.

Probably no single industry has reached the development that the automobile has, considering the fact that its activities are not quite twenty years old.

It has truly been the talk of the world. Its advancement has been rapid. The progress made from year to year has been astounding and it has engaged some of the most brilliant mechanical minds of two continents.

Today, the industry represents millions and millions of dollars.

Much money has been made not only by

those who have manufactured meritorious products, but by the army of men who have sold cars to the consumer.

Are there opportunities today? Many, indeed.

As in any other field of endeavor, much depends on the man himself. The measure of success he achieves will be in proportion to his effort and the standard by which he does business. There are certain definite rules relative to this work, that, if followed, cannot help but be beneficial to those acting on the advice given in this book.

There are opportunities in every branch of the business.

There is plenty of room for good salesmen, a lot of it, in fact.

There is room for garagemen, for dealers, and for all who have a desire to work faithfully and who are willing to attend to the duties in hand and make every effort to secure the maximum results.

Fortunes have been made in a short time in the retail field.

Money has been made and is now being made in the wholesale distribution of automobiles.

Salesmen, men who attend to business and who try to find out all about the details of successful automobile selling, are making money. No matter what branch you contemplate entering, there are plenty of opportunities providing you concentrate and do business according to the standards demanded of the successful business man of today.

The business has not altogether been ideal, but better automobile days are coming.

The time is not far off when the relationship between the factory, dealer and consumer is going to change for the better and this will be because the owner is going to have a better understanding of an automobile. He will understand its limitations, what to expect and what not to expect of it, and let us hope that he will take better care of his car and treat it with more consideration than he has in the past.

Since the beginning of the industry the

owner, in a certain sense, has been erroneously educated.

He has been given false ideas of what a piece of mechanism will do and has attached altogether too much sentiment to his machine. He has been given to understand that it will go on and on without care, without attention and without breakdowns. The average owner seems to forget that his car is made up of a collection of metal parts.

This idea is changing, of course, and it is time that it should. The dealer will profit by it, too, for he is the one who has suffered most by this method of selling automobiles.

* * *

H. W. Ford, President of the Saxon Motor Company, in reviewing the progress made by the automobile manufacturer, says:

"In all history probably no industry has shown such wonderfully rapid development as that of the automobile. Although the automobile business holds the distinction of progressing much more rapidly than any other line of activity, at the same time there are other industries that show quite as revolutionary an advance, though not such a rapid one.

"The progress of the automobile business is the industrial wonder of the age. With Aladdin-like speed—almost overnight compared with other products—the modern automobile, with its beauty, speed and luxury, has evolved from the unshapely, complicated, noisy vehicle of only a few years ago.

"And with all this unprecedented advance in design and construction, with all this development in the direction of far greater efficiency and economy, has come a new conception of dollar-for-dollar value in the producing of modern, up-to-the-minute motor cars."

* * *

"The purchasing power of a farmer is perpetual," says John N. Willys, well known in the manufacturing world. "He always has something he can sell at any time. He provides the necessities of life. The people in the cities need what the farmer grows. He is never out of work. He has ready money today.

"The motor car, once considered the rich man's plaything, is today known to be as practical as any other time-saving machinery. The average man, who can afford to buy the average priced motor car, will find that at the end of three years the car has paid for itself in time saved alone, to say nothing of the pleasure and recreation it has brought to himself and his friends.

"The wonderful progress in the motor car industry has brought it to a state of permanency not surpassed by any other industry in this country. The market for American cars is continually increasing, both on this side of the Atlantic and in foreign countries. The man who has once owned a motor car is never willingly without one. This is one of the main facts on which the stability of the industry is based.

"In addition to this, the number of purchasers who have never before owned a car is increasing. The farmer, the doctor, the real estate agent, business and professional men—men of all lines of endeavor have awakened to the realization that the money invested in a car pays big dividends in time saved, health and recreation."

* * *

"Some one has said that the automobile business offers the opportunity for the opportunist," says E. R. Benson, Vice-President of the Studebaker Corporation, in discussing this question.

"Here is a commodity which has practically a universal demand.

"Everybody wants an automobile and everyone is a prospect because almost everyone sooner or later will have a thousand dollars to spend for a good automobile. The possibilities of the automobile from a sales standpoint today are really wonderful.

"There are less than two million automobiles in the United States, which means one to every fifty people.

"In many parts of the United States there is one automobile to every twenty people. The ratio varies in all parts of the United States and it does not vary in relation to wealth per capita, to individual production ability, or to any other one thing which may be settled upon as directly responsible.

"When hard times come, it is said that the automobile business does not feel the depression as do other industries. This is true for any one of several reasons, but it is chiefly true because the merchandising saturation is not sufficiently developed to affect representative conditions. In other words, the people who are buying automobiles now are the people who can usually well afford them—the kind of people who are not greatly influenced by financial depressions.

"When automobile merchandising approaches saturation, then we will be selling cars to people who are buying them with money, which under other conditions, they would spend for more urgent necessities.

"This is a more or less roundabout way of getting at the fact that we have not begun to approach the possibilities of this business.

"Then there must be golden opportunities in this business when we can secure business today without 'intensive' sales effort, and this in reference to the pleasure car business only.

"So far as the commercial car business is concerned, we have not even begun to approach merchandising possibilities. We haven't done so much in this as we have in the pleasure car field. The commercial car and the tractor are opportunities which remain for a coming generation. Therefore, I think that I am safe in saying that the opportunities in this business are greater perhaps than they are in any other in the merchandising world today."

CHAPTER II

CHOICE OF TERRITORY

The most important thing to consider, providing you contemplate going in the business, is the location.

"Just where can I make some money in this business?"

Your first thought will probably be that with this country with hundred millions of people distributed over a wide area, it is possible to make money anywhere, but you will find upon investigation, that certain parts offer more returns than others.

To give you food for thought, there are enumerated below the names of the five most important States in the country having the largest number of car owners.

At the time this is being written, New York leads with a total number of 168,039 cars, Illinois is second with 132,199, California third with 122,625, Pennsylvania fourth with 122,071 and Iowa fifth with a total of 106,250 machines.

It will be noticeable from this that a majority of cars are owned in rich agricultural States. Thousands and thousands of small cars are owned by farmers everywhere, but especially is it true in the territory above mentioned.

There are 33,000 Fords owned in Illinois, 36,000 of them in Iowa and over 25,000 in the State of California.

Rich agricultural districts will always be safe places to locate in, for there is always going to be a certain percentage of new business, and you must not forget that there are many thousands of cars that require attention everywhere, and that there are many thousands who are always ready to make a "trade deal."

The cities, likewise, offer opportunities providing, of course, it is possible to secure proper location, or, better still, to purchase an established business. It is true that it takes money to secure advantageous locations and considerable capital to start a business, but if this can be done, it offers returns in proportion to the investment.

The field is not overcrowded anywhere. The industry is still young and there is plenty of room for those who are willing to work.

The rich agricultural States should receive your first consideration in the matter of deciding on a place to do business. Iowa, Illinois, the Dakotas, Nebraska, Missouri, Kansas, New York and Pennsylvania are uniformly good. The southern States have not been good automobile States but they promise to be better from now on. Industrial conditions have not been very good, but the whole southern territory is showing a decided improvement. Those who contemplate locating in the South should investigate with great care the district in which they intend to do business.

You can, with considerable accuracy, estimate in advance the amount of business there is likely to be in any county or group of counties. It is easy enough to ascertain the wealth and the standing of any community. In this way you will be able to judge the purchasing power of its people.

Cities having a population of twenty-five thousand and upward and being situated in rich agricultural districts are usually safe places in which to do business.

Location is all-important.

And most fortunate is the dealer who sees to it that the line he handles is adaptable to the largest number of probable buyers in the territory he covers. Here is a most important thing for you to remember. Your common sense will tell you that it would be impossible for you to make any money selling exclusively a three or four thousand dollar car in a town of three thousand, even if it had a surrounding country having automobile purchasing power, so it is well to choose a balanced line— one that will fit in with the territory in which you do business.

CHAPTER III

ORGANIZATION

In the organization of a new business be methodical in everything you do. A right beginning is most important. Plan according to the capital you intend to invest. Appropriate an amount for showroom fixtures, garage equipment, sample cars to be purchased, advertising, and other details. Start right. Do not neglect anything. Do not think that you will be a successful business man if you start without advertising, without garage equipment or without being able to display the cars properly. Because you won't. This last reference applies more to dealers selling cars above the thousand dollar mark. Many dealers are making money in the rural districts selling low-priced cars who have hardly any place of business at all.

Do not overdo in the beginning. Do not start in with extraordinary expenses. It is all right to add to your expenses as your business increases, and to use an expression now much in use, "Watch your step." It is much safer to start moderately and grow steadily, than it is to begin with a "Hurrah" and collapse suddenly.

Keep in touch with all branches of your business. Divide it into several departments even though you have only one man to handle each division.

Keep at your fingers' ends the knowledge of conditions in your garage, the results obtained by your retail salesmen, your road men and wholesale men, and, most vital of all, accurate knowledge of the financial standing of your business.

Keep in available form information of every nook and corner of your territory. Know exactly how your campaign to sell each prospect stands.

Methods should be devised to obtain and retain this information. And card files are the most practical and inexpensive means to this end. Too much time should not be expended upon them, but they should not be kept up in a half-hearted way. Inaccurate or incomplete records are not much better than no records at all.

Your prospect list is the only material you have to work with in the selling end of your business. It should be kept and guarded as valuable material would be. Just consider that each one of those names has cost you a definite sum of money.

Get all the information you can about each prospect; know just when you or your men have called upon him; just what literature he has received; the letters you have written him; why he has not purchased.

A card of the type shown herewith should be used as a permanent record and daily reports should be made on other cards and transferred to this permanent file. On the reverse side of the card are listed dates of calls, results of each, literature mailed and miscellaneous remarks.

Automobile Business

REPORT ON INDIVIDUAL PROSPECTS

Name _____ Phone No. _____

Town _____ County _____ State _____

Business Address _____ Residence Address _____

Present Business _____

Is He a Prospect _____ Reputation—Good _____ Fair _____ Poor _____

Financial Ability _____

Model Interested in _____

Price Quoted _____ Demonstration Appointment _____

What Appeals to Him Most in Car _____

How Much of a Family _____

What is His Hobby _____

Bank Report _____ Salesman _____ Rating _____

(over)

After completing one call, decide if possible the time of the next call and list it for that date. Require your men to map out definite work to accomplish each day, but do not dictate to them how to handle their individual prospects. If they do not know how, they have no right to the name *salesman*. Allow each man a definite day or two in the salesroom.

Traveling men should report each day to their home office, sending in a card for each concern or man called upon, using a form as follows, or something similar.

Town	State	Date

Firm Name _____ Credit _____

Corp. or Partnership _____

Names of Officers or Partners _____

_____

In Other Business? _____

Has Contract With _____

_____

Annual Sales _____

Interested in Our Line for Next Year _____

_____ Salesman

On the back of this card is space for special reports. One card for each name should be kept in a permanent file and the periodic reports of the salesmen recorded on the card. The cards should be filed under towns and the names in alphabetical order under this classification. Each salesman should be required to call upon every dealer in every town each time he makes that town and turn in a report. If this is done and the reports are carefully transferred, the older the file is the more valuable it will become. This also affords a good check upon your traveling men.

If you employ a number of men, have general gatherings occasionally. Have your garage men meet your salesmen. They can learn from each other. At these meetings, take up in detail the car you are selling, your competitor's car, sales methods, individual prospects, etc. Let each profit by the suggestions of the others.

* * *

R. D. Chapin, President of the Hudson Motor Car Company, has this to say on the subject of organization:

"This is the age of machinery. Machinery for selling things as well as for making them.

Mental machinery as well as things coming under the popular understanding of the word.

"The time has passed when handwork on a big sale is effective. Today everything is done by machinery.

"The time has also passed when individual efforts make a business. Today we need selling machinery—organization.

"One man cannot create a big business. One man cannot carry on a highly successful motor-car selling agency.

"Merchandising now is as complex as is manufacturing. Machinery and system will accomplish more than mere men. Though, of course, selling calls for the human element even more than does making.

"The typewriter, the telephone and the telegraph are all needed in modern merchandising. Salesmen no longer magnify the personal equation. System and plan count for more than do individuals.

"Scientific business architecture is a profession of the minute. It is perhaps the youngest of all merchandising efforts. It aims at a structure harmonious in its every part. It is based on the modern conception of scientific management.

"Buying costs, and operating costs, and selling costs all must fit together into a completed whole. Negligence anywhere in the entire system is felt instantly in the profit and loss account.

"The salesman out on the road is no more important than is the worker at the desk. The highly specialized expert must show a profit and so must the porter who sweeps the floor and washes the windows.

"Each department must be a link in the chain. Yet each must be a unit itself.

"The perfect organization is a chain of many links, each equal in strength and in the support it gives to the entire structure.

"To put these basic elements into practical and concrete form is the easiest part of the undertaking. The plan is the biggest part of the problem. Get the foundation right and the building will follow as a matter of course."

CHAPTER IV

SELECTION OF CARS

The selection of the line or lines of cars to be handled is just as important as the location and, in a certain sense, it depends on the combination of the two to be successful.

One depends on the other.

The price of a car or cars to be handled depends a good deal on the territory you are going to cover.

Price governs the supply and demand. We know from experience that the greatest market is for cars selling just below the five hundred dollar mark. We know, also, that second in demand is a car selling from five hundred to a thousand dollars; as the price goes up, the demand decreases.

If you are going to locate in an agricultural

district, you will want to sell cars ranging in price from five hundred to fifteen hundred dollars; or the price car for which there is the largest demand.

After you have decided on your lines, the next important thing is to make up your mind as to the territory you are going to cover and actually try to do business in.

Don't ask for too much territory.

You will get it, eventually, if you show that you are able to secure the business. Many dealers make the mistake of asking factories for more than they can properly work and if they make a poor showing usually lose the car they represent, for factories demand that every county in a dealer's contract be worked.

Work thoroughly whatever territory is under your control. Do not neglect any of it. Cover every corner of it. Do not let a town go by. Do not let a village go by. This is the only way to be able to get the maximum business. Do not forget that there is some business everywhere.

Feel sure of the stability of the company, or companies, you contemplate representing.

Choose companies that you know for a certainty are going to stay in business indefinitely. The safest way is to choose strong companies—those that are financially strong.

Choose companies that believe in national advertising, for this, in a great measure, will assist you.

You must select the highest quality car having the proper price in order to fit the largest number of purchasers in the territory you are doing business in.

It is a mistake to take on too many lines. Success is in concentration.

Unless you are in a position to secure the selling rights of a car selling under $750—or a machine that will permit you to devote your whole time and which will guarantee a money-making income, it would be well for you to secure the agency for two and not more than three good cars. But, in so doing, keep in mind your territory and what will sell the best.

In selecting a line or lines be guided by these things: The two most important items, and they are equally vital, are looks and mechanical dependability. You must have both, unless the car is cheap, and then the appearance is not so important.

Today, it is almost impossible to sell a car that is good mechanically and is without good looks.

Do not try it.

It was all right years ago, but it cannot be done now. And that is because women have so much to do in deciding the selection—and a woman is first of all impressed by appearances.

Next to the two items mentioned, it is well to consider riding qualities, comfort, accessibility, equipment. Give all these matters your earnest attention. It will pay you eventually.

There are certain companies in this country who are known to be in the front of the industry—those who take the lead in improvements and in giving the most for the money—

those are the companies to represent, providing it is possible.

Select companies that you know have a "fair and square" service policy—who will give you a hearing at all times and listen to your demands with some consideration.

If it is possible, be sure to visit the factory before becoming the representative. By doing this you will get some idea of the personnel of the organization and the factory itself.

You will be able to judge by this method their permanency and responsibility.

You will be able to tell by the appearance of the plant, executives, the type of men employed and the equipment whether it is a concern you want to represent.

A car is no better than the men producing it. Do not forget that.

Cars represent the ideals of the individuals making them. Take all these things into consideration before making your selections.

* * *

Considerable money is being made in selling accessories in connection with that of automobiles. This is especially true if you are doing business in towns located on important roads and having considerable through traffic.

The establishment of a department like this does not mean that it will be necessary to make a large additional investment, for if you happen to be located near wholesale supply houses you are in a position to renew your stock often.

You will find upon investigation, that you will be able to buy quite an assortment for a little money.

Do not carry unreliable accessories, for it is likely to do you considerable harm. Sell reliable goods no matter how small the article may be. Do not jeopardize your future business relations with a man by selling him an unreliable spark plug or anything else. He is not going to forget you if his small purchase proves unworthy.

There is always room for one supply man in any town, regardless of size, and it is well to investigate this matter fully when deciding on a location.

Do not load up on articles that you know little about. Do not carry in stock accessories that are not often called for. Enter into this branch of the work carefully and then you will not lose any money in the wrong selection of goods nor in overstocking.

CHAPTER V

SHOWROOM—LOCATION—WINDOWS

If you were going to buy a $50 suit of clothes, where would you go for it?

Would you go into some second-hand store on a side street, in some broken-down place? A store where the windows had not been washed in a year?

No, you would not.

You would pick out a place where you knew you would receive $50 worth of clothes, where the merchant was trustworthy. You would buy where the surroundings were good, you would buy as much reputation, location and service as you would clothes.

Men who buy automobiles figure the same way.

Have your place of business stand for the best principles.

Showroom Location

Have it stand for the best in the automobile world.

Have the environment, the atmosphere, the salesmen, the general appearance, reflect a high product.

Your merchandise is judged by its location, by its store, by the general appearance of the place.

Automobiles, in a certain sense, are judged by the men who sell them.

Your men reflect the car.

As an actor needs a beautiful piece of scenery to set off his work on the stage, so do cars need a good background to set off all the beauty and elegance they may possess. Have your cars look smart all the time.

There is an old saying "A man is known by the company he keeps," and in a certain sense this is true in the automobile business. A car is known by the company it keeps, who sells it, where it is sold and how it is sold.

You cannot be too particular about the looks of your showroom. Watch the little things and watch them all the time.

Don't get a "spell on" and look after the cleanliness and appearance of the place for a week and then neglect it the balance of the month. Keep after it.

Keep the windows clean. Wash them every day if necessary, but keep them clean. You wouldn't think that this suggestion is necessary but it is, just the same.

Unless you are showing the motor, keep the hood down. Nothing so detracts from the looks of a car as a hood sticking up in the air. Change the position of cars on the floor every little while.

For a time, place them in such a position as will show off the radiator to best advantage. Let the people get acquainted with the front of the car you sell.

Keep the cars looking "in the pink of condition." Have the caretaker go over them often. Remember, a prospect gets his first impression of a car by seeing it on the showroom floor. You can see to it that this impression is right by having your cars look *right*.

Watch for finger-marks on bodies and for dust on the fenders and spokes. Keep the nickel parts looking bright. Satisfy yourself that the cars could not look better.

Set a high standard for your showroom and it will make a favorable impression on the man who comes into your place for the first time. Let him notice that you are a modern business man and up to the minute in every way. It will inspire confidence.

* * *

Department stores spend thousands of dollars annually in their windows. The average motor-car dealer leaves the window of his salesroom empty. The average garage owner fills his window with a conglomeration of junk.

Thousands of people pass your place of business and never give you a thought. You have practically unlimited "circulation"—provided your location is good—and you waste it.

Take an example from the hustling newsboy. First he shouts his ware. You can't do that literally—although that, figuratively speaking, is just what you do when you advertise.

Second, he thrusts his paper under your eyes so you can't fail to read the headlines. You can do the same.

You can make a window display so striking that it compels attention. It halts the casual passerby and thrusts your story under his eyes. He cannot help but read your message in the window if it is properly presented. And he cannot help but carry a good impression away with him.

To continue the newspaper parallel, heed the example of the headlines. Make your window tell your story concisely. Headlines are in big type to attract attention—make your window display striking. Let it have unity.

It is true that it is difficult to work up an inexpensive window display with an automobile. But, it can be done.

Try and present the unusual. An automobile placed where it can be seen through the window does not mean anything, particularly to the passerby. He can turn around and see hundreds, to his unsearching eyes, identical. But a stripped chassis is not a usual sight. It will attract a certain amount of attention for it is not seen often.

Anything moving in a window will draw crowds. Striking color combinations as backgrounds will make your display stand out. Brief explanatory cards are good. Do not overlook them.

Study lighting effects. Never allow a light to shine into the onlooker's eyes. A small amount of money expended on window lights is a good investment.

Concentrate attention upon your window. Do not permit a view of the interior of your showroom as a background detracts from the display in the window. Use some curtain or drapery as a background.

Study the advertising campaign of the factory you represent. Line up your windows with it. Display copies of advertisements simultaneously with their appearance. When your new models come out spend a little money on a big canvas sign. A glaring sign used once or twice a year to announce important events is good business. But it should not be used too frequently or its effect will be lost.

You can work wonders with a few yards of bunting, some lumber and a hammer. They are the only stock in trade of a window trimmer—plus originality.

But do not waste your windows. From the street ninety per cent. of the automobile salesrooms in smaller towns have every appearance of being a vacant store. Let people know you are alive.

* * *

The garage man, as a rule, totally ignores his windows, and for this very reason your accessory display will be doubly effective. For you will have no window-competition.

The same general rules for window dressing apply here, with special emphasis upon concentration. The dealer who does use his windows usually tries to display his entire stock, which is not necessary.

Concentrate upon one or two articles and display them with their prices. Money invested in the work of a professional sign writer is well spent.

When you display tires, tell the man who looks at them their size and price. When you show a jack, make it hold something up. When you show a tire pump, make it pump—people will stop to look at wheels going around whether the wheels accomplish anything or not.

Name your displays. Price them.

Take advantage of the advertising done by the accessory manufacturer. Many a man has been sold through having seen an advertisement, but has passed your store because you didn't tell him you had the article. If the manufacturer of a warning signal is advertising extensively, let the people know you have his signal. Watch the trade papers, general magazines, and newspapers.

Be consistent. Don't display tire repair outfits at the same time as puncture proof tires.

Use your windows. Keep them well lighted. Change them often.

* * *

In discussing the subject of location, George S. Waite of the Grant Motor Company, says:

"A great deal has been written and much more has been said upon this vital thing, and about as many opinions exist as there are men in the business. Therefore, in giving my authoritative opinion, I am taking a leap into the darkness, with the full knowledge that my ideas will probably be shot to pieces by a number of authorities scattered through the United States.

"But to get down to brass tacks—I have had in charge showroom locations in New York, Boston, Cleveland, and numerous other centers, and my observations lead me to believe that a desirable corner location on a desirable street, not necessarily on 'Automobile Row,' but one with modern show windows and proper lighting, is the only location to make to display your wares attractively. In contradiction to this statement, a great many successful retailers of automobiles have made their mark and secured their business on side streets, overcoming the manifest disadvantage of a side-street location by the proper conduct of their business. And by proper conduct, I mean a carefully kept, clean, wholesome salesroom. This, to my way of thinking, is essential.

"The salesroom on the prominent corner is absolutely of no advantage, provided the conditions within this salesroom are not correct. In other words, a corner salesroom with dirty windows, poorly kept floors, a slack display of cars, and salesmen smoking cigarettes and gossiping with one another, will absolutely make that salesroom of no value, in spite of its location, whereas the fellow on the side street, with conditions diametrically opposed to those mentioned, will make a huge success.

"In conclusion, the location of a salesroom is of secondary importance to the manner in which it is conducted. Success does not follow location. It is only a combination of efficiency in the sales organization and salesroom itself, which will produce the largest amount of business."

CHAPTER VI

SALESMEN

The most important thing in any business is in the selection of salesmen.

Do not neglect this important matter.

It is so vital, that the difference between good and poor salesmanship might mean the difference between a money-making year and a losing one.

A good salesman is a precious jewel; a poor one, the most unprofitable investment you can make, even if he does not cost you much money.

In selecting salesmen, be guided by these three important points. Measure them carefully and see to it that they come up to this standard: (*a*) Ability; (*b*) Reliability; (*c*) Endurance.

Ability: Convince yourself of the appli-

"In conclusion, the location of a salesroom is of secondary importance to the manner in which it is conducted. Success does not follow location. It is only a combination of efficiency in the sales organization and salesroom itself, which will produce the largest amount of business."

CHAPTER VI

SALESMEN

The most important thing in any business is in the selection of salesmen.

Do not neglect this important matter.

It is so vital, that the difference between good and poor salesmanship might mean the difference between a money-making year and a losing one.

A good salesman is a precious jewel; a poor one, the most unprofitable investment you can make, even if he does not cost you much money.

In selecting salesmen, be guided by these three important points. Measure them carefully and see to it that they come up to this standard: (*a*) Ability; (*b*) Reliability; (*c*) Endurance.

Ability: Convince yourself of the appli-

His words gave the article a new meaning. You forgot he was describing a little mechanical contrivance. You forgot he was selling the dullest sort of a thing, for he made you see the object from his standpoint.

His voice sounded true, also. He evidently believed what he was saying. Thus he was impressive. He was "wrapped up" in his subject. And he never left it for a moment. He just talked business.

We saw him several weeks later in Detroit.

He was still at it. He hadn't lost a bit of his enthusiasm, energy or vitality.

His plea—his argument—his selling talk—was just as fresh as when we heard it for the first time. To hear him, it would have occurred to you that it was his first day on the job. He was so glowing, so convincing, so sure of what he was saying.

That's the kind of salesmanship that wins.

It is necessary to put action, life and energy into the words uttered and the face must interpret the speech. Look earnest.

Let us not forget for a single moment that

like the actor on the stage, the salesman must be consistent in performance.

The salesman must not vary in the power of his solicitation.

He must do the very best he knows how each time.

For in the end it spells "Victory." Nothing short of this can possibly win.

CHAPTER VII

SALESMANSHIP AND THE PROSPECT

Salesmanship, as applied to the selling of automobiles, may be divided into several parts. But as in any other business, there are certain fundamentals that should govern those who wish to achieve maximum success in this business.

It does not require any lengthy training to fit one to become an automobile salesman. It is simply necessary to master the construction of one car, for in general, the building plan that applies to one is applicable to all. There are details in which one car differs from another, but it does not require much time to master them.

Knowledge of motor-car construction is the first requisite. Some argue that it is not essential by pointing out salesmen who are successful, but have no technical learning. But it is better to be on the safe side, especially as it does not take much time to become thoroughly acquainted with the function of each unit, and the application of one part to another.

It is not hard for the average layman to gain, in a short time, the information necessary for a general understanding of chassis construction.

The motor, of course, supplies the power; the clutch, which is usually next in line, connects the motor with the unit called the transmission which regulates the speeds, and the transmission is connected on to the driving shaft, which in turn fits on by a pinion to the rear axle.

Knowledge of the manufacture of a car is a good thing to have, because it makes you feel sure of yourself.

Knowledge on your part invites confidence. For an example: You are speaking to a prospective purchaser. He says, "Mr. Salesman, how many and what kind of bearings are used in the rear axle?" Suppose you should answer, "Mr. Prospective Purchaser, I don't know." He would come to the conclusion that you didn't know much about your car, and as a result might lose interest in it and would from then on underestimate anything you might say in its behalf.

So invite confidence by having at your finger-tips every detail relating to the car or cars you are selling.

A writer on business topics makes use of the phrase, "Educated enthusiasm" as applied to successful business and salesmanship. Let us interpret it from an automobile selling standpoint. First dividing the phrase and dealing with the word "educated."

"Educated" means that you should know your subject thoroughly—know the car by heart—the construction—the advantages of the particular way of building—the individuality of the design—the beauty of the body—the finish—the upholstering and other details.

You cannot very well feel genuinely enthusiastic about a thing unless you have

Salesmanship and the Prospect 49

reasons for it—that's where the "educated part" of salesmanship comes in.

"Enthusiasm" is the genuine feeling you should have after you have educated yourself on the subject and compared your product with that of others on the market. And "educated enthusiasm" is so vital and necessary to have if a salesman is to be a "top notcher"—a leader—a front-row man.

And so "educated enthusiasm" means knowing your subject by heart and from every angle, and being genuinely enthusiastic over the car because it represents to your mind (you being a salesman) the best product on the market. It is simply a question of being sold on the proposition before you are able to convince others.

Sell the car to yourself—it will be easy after that.

* * *

Don't mind what competitors say of your car.

If they have their hammers out it's a good sign that they are worrying about it.

People don't knock about anything unless it worries them.

Knocking is a form of spite—knocking is a disease—a peculiar mental condition. A good salesman should never get the habit.

It's bad—for it poisons the mind.

And don't forget either, that the old saying, "Every knock is a boost," is still apt.

Knocking belongs to the dark ages—let it remain there.

We don't believe knocking ever got anybody anything. The moment you knock you belittle yourself—and what you have to sell.

Mind your own business.

Sell a thing on its merits—sell the car you handle on its merits.

* * *

Meet a man with a smile on your face.

It is a good opening. A smile invites another smile. And aside from that, it usually suggests a pleasant thought.

And if you can do that, you have your man in a receptive mood.

When a man walks into your store, see to it that he is spoken to promptly and pleasantly. We all like to receive attention, and so do not spoil the introduction by neglecting anyone who comes into your place of business.

There are all sorts of prospects—no two are alike.

At the same time, there are natural laws which each man is susceptible to and the purpose of this chapter is to give you some thoughts and ideas in which all buyers are interested.

The eye has always been the first to be satisfied.

It does not make any difference whether a man is buying a necktie, a shirt, a suit of clothes or an automobile; if he is impressed with the appearance of the thing he wants, you have made a very important impression, so it is a good thing to dwell, for some time, on the appearance of your car—especially if there is a woman present.

Don't talk price to a man until you have

to—providing he does not bring up the subject first.

The most important thing to do is to interest the prospect by telling him the details and advantages of the car in question.

Get him interested—vitally so—and then, the price will not have the same effect providing he had a cheaper car in mind.

We all know that first impressions are most important.

A man will look at a car—take it in at first glance—and he gets his first impression—it's either good or bad—all depending on his mind and his personal likes.

Now then, supposing the first impression is good, it is then time to give him the details and good points—and then the price.

The point brought out here has happened to us all.

We look at a thing and we like it. "It's just the thing we want," we say—and we ask the price—and then we shudder a minute. We ask to be shown something cheaper. We see it—but we do not like it. Our mind goes

Salesmanship and the Prospect

back to the first impression—the thing we saw first and liked—and we usually buy it—if it is not out of reach of our pocketbook.

It is the same way with a number of automobile buyers.

So see to it that the first impression is good.

Get your prospect behind the wheel.

This will start him on a new line of thought. He will think of mastering the car—of driving it—of making the car go as fast as he wants to—anywhere—any time. Impress him with these points.

Don't say anything about the mechanical part of the car unless the prospect shows an inclination to discuss that part of it. Mechanical talks usually lead to confusion and argument, and that's what you want to avoid.

However, if he does show a disposition to talk of the mechanical side, use your most important points.

Be sure and tell the prospect about exclusive features. Nothing so pleases a man or woman in these days of social rivalry, as to be told that you are offering something new—an exclusive feature not found on any other car.

The careful salesman studies each prospect.

Weigh each word uttered by him—and you will not have any trouble in ascertaining just what he wants—and then it is up to you to bring out conspicuously the very things he has been talking about—you must show him that your car has all of them.

If your prospect shows an inclination to discuss mechanical and other details, go right along, just as if you were glad to be given the opportunity of going into the matter so completely.

Start in with the motor. Explain to him the important points of construction. Point out the advantages it contains. Show him how power waste is eliminated—how friction is eliminated—how vibration is eliminated. Show him the particular construction which tends to greater general efficiency and increased power.

Salesmanship and the Prospect

Be sure and impress upon him the simplicity of the chassis and how it is divided into units. Point out how very little power is lost between the motor, clutch, transmission and the driving shaft.

Point out the position of the starting button—the sight feed—the various devices and their uses, and each item which would give the prospect an idea of the completeness of the car.

Point out to him the comfortable riding position. Show him with what ease he can reach the emergency brake and the change-speed lever.

After you have finished showing him the front seats, show him the tonneau and have him test the cushions and the comfort of the rear seats.

Aside from any questions he may ask you, it is well to point out the safety of the steering gear, the large braking surface and the advantages of the type of spring suspension employed. Make it a point to tell him that it is almost impossible to "turn turtle," owing to the low center of gravity and that for the same reason, skidding is virtually done away with. Safety is an important point to the new and nervous drivers (reading of accidents, etc.) and sometimes this very thing will help close a sale.

After you have finished the mechanical end of your sales talk, turn your attention to the discussion of exclusive features.

It is true, indeed, that many sales are decided on little things. The writer knows of an instance where a car was sold on the spot because the woman liked the cut-glass robe rail in the tonneau of a seven-passenger touring car. You want to think of these little things, and they should be played up when necessary. You are able to judge your prospects and you can usually tell just what will appeal in each case.

When speaking with a prospective purchaser look earnest; and have your facial expression interpret your very language. The earnest man, when he talks earnestly, looks that way. Convey by your manner and tone of voice that you really believe what you are saying.

Reach for a man's pocketbook through his mind.

You must win him with your arguments, just as a lawyer wins over a jury by his speech.

Here is the thought to keep in mind:

That a sale is a match between two minds. When you attempt to sell a man something, you are trying to master his mind by making him believe what you are saying relative to the article you are trying to sell him.

You must be convincing, earnest and resourceful.

The man who swings the buyer's mind his way, is going to land the order.

Do not let a man put you off. It's a subject he does not throw off quickly and is apt to decide any moment, especially if a number of automobile men are after him.

Do not neglect a prospect. Pay special attention to every name received by you from the factory you represent. These names cost money, for they usually represent answers to advertisements. And so you should put forth every effort to close a sale.

It is true that some of the inquiries are not of any value, that is, there are those who write for catalogs who do not have any intention of buying cars—who have no purchasing power. But the majority of those requesting catalogs mean business, and no time should be lost in seeing them.

Do not neglect the man who comes into your place of business and says that he is just "looking around," for he is likely to be more serious than the fellow who tells you rather loudly that "he is in the market for a car and is going to buy right away."

The man who "gum shoes" into your place, and who is the meekest, is usually the man with the ready money—but he doesn't want you to know it—because he is the type who wants "dollar for dollar" value, and makes it a point to canvass the market most thoroughly in the price class he intends purchasing. He is the man who has the

Salesmanship and the Prospect

"Missouri" way with him no matter where he was born. His life slogan is "Show me."

And you had better make up your mind that you have to do it the moment you talk with this class of prospects. If he has his wife with him, you must be sure to convince her with equal force—because he won't dare to say "Yes" until she does.

The writer remembers distinctly a certain dialogue between a salesman and a prospective purchaser. The deal was apparently closed—all except the decision on the color scheme. The salesman had a brewster green car on the floor and he was anxious to sell it. He waxed eloquent in its favor, explaining to the prospect the popularity of the color, the durability, the good taste and many other things.

This was carried on for about ten minutes, when the buyer said: "Wait a minute, I'll call my wife up."

He did. And then the trouble started. Would she have a brewster green? She would not. No, indeed. She wanted a special color, of course. And in the end, she had her way. The sale was made—but the woman in the case won her point and her color was chosen.

Never argue with a woman prospect. It never pays. And if you do, you stand a good chance of losing a sale. Agree with her in everything she says, but do not fail to find a way to tell her your side of the story and make every effort to convince her that you are right, but in such a way as not to offend her.

A prospect passes through various stages before he makes his purchase, and patience is sometimes required on your part when dealing with him. There are times when it is well to press decision; but it all depends on the individual. It has been figured out that the mind works in this order when in the act of selection and buying: Attention, Interest, Desire, Conviction and Action. In a good many cases little time lapses between these stages, but it is easy enough to see that, if only for a minute, the mind registers and passes all these stages. Here, then, is something for you to remember and watch over and use to your advantage.

Every buyer is interested in maintenance cost; this, of course, includes gasoline consumption, and it is well to be thoroughly posted on these two items. Be able to prove specific cases. Make it a point to secure letters from owners in your territory, bearing out your statements relative to these two points. The stronger you can make your case in this respect, the better off you will be, because, to the average owner these two questions are of vital importance, and his decision, in a measure, will be based on the showing different cars make in this respect.

* * *

"We hear a lot today about the 'Psychology of Salesmanship,'" says J. V. Hall, General Sales Manager of the Olds Motor Works. "Some of it is sense and a lot of it is nonsense. The sensible part of it merely is an attempt to analyze and explain the processes which ordinarily take place in the prospect's mind from the time he notices your product to the time the sale is closed. The salesman who knows enough of practical psychology to be able to follow these successive changes of mind through which his prospect passes as a sale progresses, also knows the *right thing to say at the right time.*

"His remarks are timely and to the point, because he is keenly following the mental changes his prospect is experiencing, and is able to shape and direct the changes to his advantage by the right selling talk. He neither forces the sale too fast nor does he allow it to drag, but develops it intelligently and naturally.

"Every customer who buys a motor car goes through certain mental changes which may be classified as follows:

"His attention must first be called to the car in a way that will impress him favorably. This may be accomplished by magazine or newspaper advertising, by correspondence, by window display, by seeing the car on the street, by statements from a friend or by a personal call from the salesman.

"Securing a list of prospects means simply getting a list of people whose attention has been or may be favorably attracted to your car. The prospect file is of the greatest importance (it is the raw material out of which the salesman must manufacture his finished product). Every sales organization must be constantly gathering, classifying and following up prospects. If this is not done, it will be in the same position as a factory which has insufficient raw material on which to work—its efforts, instead of being well organized and intelligently directed, will be scattered, spasmodic and inefficient.

"Calling attention to a car helps to make the uninterested a prospect, but seldom does it make a purchaser. The prospect must be followed up. His *interest* must be aroused. This is the next step in the selling process and is most effectively accomplished by a personal call from the salesman. In cases where this is not possible, resort must be had to printed matter and correspondence. The selling argument at this point should be strong but brief and confined to striking points, easily understood, which make an impression quickly but do not confuse with details that should come later.

"Every salesman should have a detailed and technical knowledge of his car, but this knowledge should be imparted only when the prospect is ready for it. His interest should first be stimulated by a few clear, strong, statements about the essential and impressive qualities of the car.

"Once the interest of the prospect in the car has been aroused, the next step is to make him want it. His interest may be merely curiosity at first, having in it no element of real desire to possess the car for his own use. At this stage the salesman's technical knowledge of the fine points of his product will come into play.

"The beauty of the car, its distinction of line and design, its comfort and riding qualities, its refinements of detail, the power and flexibility of the motor and the mechanical perfection throughout—all these and many

Salesmanship and the Prospect

like points should be presented, with the emphasis on those things which appeal most strongly to the particular prospect, in an effort to make him want the car because he believes it superior to any other he can get.

"Little, if anything, should be said about price at this stage.

"Rather the talk should be of the quality and excellence of the features in which the prospect has displayed the most interest.

"Satisfy him of the superior merit of your car and he will want it.

"Once the real desire to own it is aroused, the talk will lead naturally and easily to price, and to comparison of your price with those of competitors, which comparison you need not fear, because you have had a chance to drive home to the prospect the excellence and value of your car and he is in a state of mind to consider price intelligently and without prejudice to your proposition.

"The prospect now wants the car.

"Desire for it has been created. He is beginning to think of actually buying. His next thought will be: 'Can I rely absolutely on what the salesman has told me?' This is the stage in the progress of the sale when you must be absolutely sure of yourself, where any hesitancy or doubt, or conflicting statements will injure your chance of success.

"Don't talk glittering generalities and make wild, bombastic assertions, but put all the honest enthusiasm you are capable of behind your arguments, which should be solidly based on a thorough knowledge of the car. You are now talking price also, preparatory to closing, but always back up your price talk with quality talk. Never lose sight of the fact that whatever price the prospect is considering, the price you are making is an honest one. Once you have convinced the prospect that the statements you have made to him are facts and you have established yourself in his confidence, you are ready to put the "closing punch" in your argument.

"Many a sale has been lost at this point, because the salesman lacked the moral courage, the enthusiasm and the power of personality to force the sale to completion and to close it up.

"Some salesmen will skillfully pilot a prospect through the preliminary stages up to the point where the definite decision to buy must be made, and then lose their grip, get nervous, temporize and muss up the whole thing.

"When the prospect is ripe for closing with, muster all the quiet confidence there is in you and *close*.

"Help him to jump the narrow ditch that divides prospects from purchasers.

"The ditch isn't wide and with the running start gained through bringing him successfully through all the preliminary steps, the jump should be easy.

"Don't do all the hard work of climbing up the hill until you are almost at the top and then fall down and roll to the bottom again. Cultivate closing ability, learn to do it tactfully, naturally, gracefully, firmly, but above all *do it*.

"Application is the prime element determining a salesman's success or failure.

next thought will be: 'Can I rely absolutely on what the salesman has told me?' This is the stage in the progress of the sale when you must be absolutely sure of yourself, where any hesitancy or doubt, or conflicting statements will injure your chance of success.

"Don't talk glittering generalities and make wild, bombastic assertions, but put all the honest enthusiasm you are capable of behind your arguments, which should be solidly based on a thorough knowledge of the car. You are now talking price also, preparatory to closing, but always back up your price talk with quality talk. Never lose sight of the fact that whatever price the prospect is considering, the price you are making is an honest one. Once you have convinced the prospect that the statements you have made to him are facts and you have established yourself in his confidence, you are ready to put the "closing punch" in your argument.

"Many a sale has been lost at this point, because the salesman lacked the moral courage, the enthusiasm and the power of personality to force the sale to completion and to close it up.

"Some salesmen will skillfully pilot a prospect through the preliminary stages up to the point where the definite decision to buy must be made, and then lose their grip, get nervous, temporize and muss up the whole thing.

"When the prospect is ripe for closing with, muster all the quiet confidence there is in you and *close*.

"Help him to jump the narrow ditch that divides prospects from purchasers.

"The ditch isn't wide and with the running start gained through bringing him successfully through all the preliminary steps, the jump should be easy.

"Don't do all the hard work of climbing up the hill until you are almost at the top and then fall down and roll to the bottom again. Cultivate closing ability, learn to do it tactfully, naturally, gracefully, firmly, but above all *do it*.

"Application is the prime element determining a salesman's success or failure.

"Ninety per cent. of failures are due simply to lack of hard work. Lack of hard work fires any salesman, no matter how clever he may be.

"Hard work brings results.

"Hard work makes for success. Many salesmen, so-called, studiously comb prospect files, make lead-pencil notes, refer hourly to little memorandum books, ride back and forth on street cars—unfortunately sometimes in automobiles—do considerable bluff talking over the telephone and walk about with a hurried look of assumed business importance. *This is not work.*

"Actual conversation with real prospective purchasers is work. The rest is preliminary frill.

"A real salesman spends just as many hours in 'Simon pure' work, and no more than can be measured by the actual time he is drilling in the merits of his product to prospective purchasers.

"If your prospective purchaser has objections, overcome them by reasoning, not by arguing.

"Many an argument has been won at the expense of the order.

"The prospective purchaser may buy from a certain salesman because he respects the salesman's judgment, but not because they are friends.

"Purchases are rarely made through friendship, and, when they are, they are often disappointing.

"If the prospective purchaser shows a desire to ask questions or raise objections, let him do so and answer the question or objection before going to another point.

"Don't be bull-headed.

"Make the prospective purchaser feel that you respect his judgment. Nothing will start opposition or antagonism more quickly than a seeming disregard for his opinions and objections.

"Convince your prospective purchaser on each point before leaving it.

"Remember it is not what you say that sells him, it is what he believes.

"It is in the economic nature of man to

barter, and since trading constitutes such a large percentage of your deals, it is vital to your interest that you talk quality and not price.

"If the prospective purchaser interrupts with price talk before you have had an opportunity to thoroughly acquaint him with the real value of the car, avoid a direct answer if possible and plunge into car quality.

"His inquiry regarding price is an acknowledgment that your first point has scored. *Some salesmen quit here.* Do not make this fatal mistake.

"Your object is to make the prospective purchaser want your car, regardless of price.

"Make price secondary."

CHAPTER VIII

CAR KNOWLEDGE

If you haven't a taste for mechanics, cultivate one.

You will find it a profitable hobby, if nothing more.

You will be surprised to learn that it does not take much time to acquire a good working knowledge of the mechanical principles of a motor car.

Following is the usual procedure in factories, as to the method of manufacturing cars:

There are two general methods followed by automobile manufacturers. Cars are built complete in the factory or factories of one company. Or, little or no actual manufacturing is done, the various units or parts being purchased from companies who specialize in their manufacture alone and being merely assembled in the plant of the company whose name the completed car bears.

Both methods have their advantages, although a car built complete by one company is generally considered the better.

With the manufactured car the procedure is as follows:

The engineering department is always a year ahead—sometimes two or three—of the production departments. The engineers and draftsmen design the car complete and specify the material to be used.

1. The purchasing department orders raw material which is:
   - (a) Analyzed to come up to engineers' specifications.
   - (b) Delivered to the foundry and castings are made.
   - (c) Or steel, iron, etc., may be received as rough stock, then it is:
   - (d) Analyzed and also tested for hardness, tensile strength, etc.
   - (e) Various parts go through drop forging plant and are stamped out.

Car Knowledge

2. Castings or forgings go to machine shop where:
   - (a) The parts which go to make up the various units are machined.
   - (b) Inspected for size, many measurements being as fine or finer than 1-1000 of an inch.
   - (c) Inspected for defects in workmanship.

3. Many parts which are subjected to unusual strains, continual wear, etc., go to the heat treating department:
   - (a) Parts are heated to high temperature and cooled scientifically to produce extreme hardness and strength.

4. Various parts are assembled into units:
   - (a) Motor.
   - (b) Clutch.
   - (c) Transmission.
   - (d) Drive shaft, with one or more universal joints.
   - (e) Front axle.
   - (f) Rear axle.

(g) Springs.
(h) Steering gear, etc.
5. Units receive various tests:
   (a) Motor is run on block so parts work together; bearings are tightened; then tested on dynamometer until it attains certain number of revolutions per minute. Tested for quietness, vibration, etc.
   (b) Clutch is tested for smooth operation.
   (c) Transmission tested for quietness.
   (d) Springs tested for resiliency.
   (e) Axles tested for strength; rear axle tested for quietness; brakes adjusted, etc.
6. Units are collected and assembled into complete chassis.
   (a) Chassis is tested on road and all necessary adjustments are made.
   (b) Chassis is thoroughly cleaned usually by means of steam jet.
   (c) Exposed parts smoothed with emery paper.

(*d*) Chassis is given several coats of paint.

7. Bodies are usually purchased from a plant specializing in this work, as are electrical equipment, carburetor, bearings, and a few other parts which few manufacturers of automobiles attempt to make.

    (*a*) Body is carefully inspected and imperfections corrected.

    (*b*) Paint, first coat.

    (*c*) Sand blast, or smoothed by hand.

    (*d*) Many priming and rough-stuff coats alternated with hand-rubbing process.

    (*e*) Final coats and finish in dust-proof rooms.

    (*f*) Striping.

8. Upholstering and tops.

    (*a*) Leather is carefully inspected and sewed to shape.

    (*b*) Hair is carefully picked.

    (*c*) Seat cushions are made separately, backs are upholstered in completed body.

(d) Top and side curtains are fitted to body.
9. Sheet metal parts are cut and shaped.
   (a) Fenders, hood, and small parts such as gear-shifting lever, etc., are dipped in enamel several times.
   (b) Finish is baked on in oven after each dipping.
   (c) Gasoline tank is painted.
10. Final assembly.
    (a) Body is fitted to chassis.
    (b) Fenders, running board, gasoline tank, etc., are fitted. All connections and attachments are made. Tires are attached.
    (c) Electrical equipment is tested.
    (d) Complete car is sent out on road test.
    (e) Adjustments are made for minor defects which road test has developed.
    (f) Final road test.

It is a good idea to know the kind of material each part is made of; how it is made; and what special claims are made for it.

Know the size of all bearings and know the location of them; the kind used in each case and why they are preferable.

Know something about wheel, body, and top construction. Be able to explain the oiling system. Know the weights of the cars. Explain the construction of the cushions. Be able to talk about each accessibility point. Find out what the exclusive features are and play them up. Know every detail of the car.

In addition, here are some things you also should know:

1. The bore and stroke of the motor.
2. The material used in construction of the following parts: Cylinders, pistons, wrist pins, connecting rods, inlet and exhaust valves, crank shaft, cam shaft, timing gears, frame, springs, front and rear axle.
3. Type of carburetor used and reasons for it.
4. Starting, lighting, and ignition systems used and selling points covering each unit.
5. Type of clutch and selling points covering it.

6. Style of steering gear used; best reasons for it. Be sure and learn the claims for safety and dependability.

7. Brakes—how they act—the lining—safety features.

SIMPLE MOTOR DEFINITIONS YOU SHOULD KNOW

The four-stroke cycle type of motor is the one commonly employed today in automobile construction.

Four-cycle means that it takes four operations (or cycle) to cause a single explosion in the cylinder. The following are the four operations:

1. Intake or introduction of gases.
2. Compression stroke (compression of gases).
3. Working stroke. (This includes the ignition and explosion.)
4. Exhaust stroke. (Expels burnt gases.)

Cylinder:

The cylinder is the principal stationary part of an engine, cylindrical in shape.

There is an opening at the bottom for the piston; a smaller opening for the admission and exhaust of gases; there is also an opening for the igniting device, or spark plug.

Piston:

The piston is a cylindrical unit which travels back and forth inside of the cylinder under the action of the explosive gases, and is fitted with rings which prevent the gases escaping from the cylinder when under compression.

Piston Ring:

A narrow ring which fits into a groove in the piston and is used for the purpose of making an air-tight fit of the piston.

Crank Case:

The crank case is a metal base which serves as a foundation for the motor, and also acts as a base for the main bearings on which the crank shaft rotates.

Crank Shaft:

The crank shaft is one of the most important parts of the gasoline motor for the reason that it transforms the reciprocating motion of the connecting rods, produced by the expansion of the gases, to a rotating motion as required to drive the rear wheels.

Valves:

Valves regulate the introduction and removal of gases and are operated mechanically.

Cams:

Cams operate the valves and are so constructed as to open and close the valves at the proper time to allow the admission and expulsion of gases.

Carburetor:

The carburetor is a device used in obtaining an explosive mixture of gasoline and air.

Ignition System:

Electric spark is used for igniting the mixture after it has reached the combustion chamber.

Cooling System:

Is the circulation of water to such parts of the motor as require cooling. This keeps the walls of the cylinders from becoming hot. For this reason cylinders are built with water-jacket compartments. Water is forced to these parts or circulates by the heat of the water. The system is usually arranged so that the water circulates from the lower part of the radiator up through the water-jackets and back to the radiator.

Transmission:

An intermediary device (usually a set of gears) used for transmitting the power from the motor to the rear or driving part of the car at different speeds.

* * *

F. E. Moskovics, of the Marmon Company, a pioneer in the industry, voices the following on this question:

"The writer deprecates too much technical information in the hands of a dealer. One reason is that this knowledge can never be thorough. If it were, he would be an engineer. Half knowledge is extremely dangerous. What the dealer should know is, first, his car. He should know this backwards and forwards. He should know the theory and reason for everything about his car.

"Next, he should know each direct competing line practically as well and should be able to point out logically, concisely, and clearly the differences and advantages of his construction. His knowledge on this score should be irrefutable. He should know exactly the capabilities of his car. What it will do on the steepest hill in his community, both fast and slow. What it will do on the level stretches, and he should know approximately what his leading competitors will do over the same roads.

"Armed with this knowledge he can either go out and conquer or know how to avoid pitfalls. In other words, I would say that the dealer must know his car, and then must know his chief competitor's car. When he has this knowledge well grounded, firmly embedded, he will avoid exaggerations and misstatements and will stick only to known facts.

"This knowledge is no easy one to gain. It takes time and study, but what dealer expects to gain success who won't put the time, energy, and study necessary to gain this knowledge?

"The above refers purely to the technical side of his business. That he should study modern merchandising and advertising and its effects upon his market is too elementary to need bring up here. I can, therefore, confine my advice to the dealer in these few words: 'Know your car; put yourself in the position that no one can ask you a reasonable question about it which you cannot answer; and next to this, know your competitor's car.'

"This will incite in a customer's mind that confidence which is credited only to those who know."

CHAPTER IX

ADVERTISING

The man who stood still is dead.

Ever hear of him?

He lived in an Illinois town. At one time a successful merchant, he refused to step along to the march of progress. He refused to grow. He refused to advertise. He became careless of his place of business. Customers left him—and he finally became a business derelict. For years he was known as the man who stood still.

What a lesson it teaches!

To be in business and be successful means to be progressive—no matter what you are selling.

Don't stand still. If you do you are going backward. If you stand still, someone else is going forward.

Why not be the man to go forward?

It all rests with you. You can be just as important as you want to, but——

You must cast aside old methods—old rules—old habits.

You must adopt twentieth century methods.

Do business according to the standards of the day.

And one of the standards demanded today is advertising.

Have you ever considered advertising as a form of business insurance?

You carry life insurance as a protection for those you love.

You should advertise as a protection for future business and to secure permanency for your name.

You should consider advertising as a form of business insurance.

Advertising, like insurance, will work for you all the time after you have once started.

Advertising will surround you with a certain asset (in the form of good will) which will result in increased business.

If you think seriously of this question, you will come to the conclusion that you should start advertising and make it a part of your business, just as much so as any branch of it, and just as quickly as you start in business.

Do not get the idea that it is money wasted simply because after you have run an advertisement or two, you do not see a lot of people flocking into your store and asking for the article that you advertise.

Advertising does not do anything as wonderful as that all the time. But its power is sure and you cannot expect one or two advertisements a year to show results.

Your advertising must be consistent.

Advertising is so important and so closely linked with the success of business that you should consider it a part of your business and pay some attention to it.

George Fitch, in one of his clever essays, says this of advertising: "Some business can get along without advertising, just as some men can make a living, although dumb, but both are uphill jobs. Advertising has kept Sarah Bernhardt young and attractive for sixty-seven years and the lack of it made Edgar Allan Poe starve at forty."

Advertising, to be successful in its purpose, must be persistent in character and methodical in appearance. You must remember, that persistent advertising creates confidence and repetition establishes reputation. Advertising performs this wonderful miracle almost unconsciously. Let us cite an example.

Take, for instance, Steinway pianos. When we think of pianos, do we not unconsciously think of the Steinway, and without any reason? It isn't because we are familiar with pianos—not because we know about the construction—not because we are judges of tone value, but because we have seen Steinway pianos advertised for years, and the name has remained with us and is associated in our minds with the very best in piano construction. Imagine, if you can, the value of the name "Steinway" as an asset alone. Think of the standing that it has in the commercial world. And what is true of this, is true of any other persistently advertised product.

If you want to grow, if you have a desire to expand, spend money in developing your name and your business.

Do it systematically—regularly. Printer's ink is such a vital force today, that to ignore it is simply to admit that you are backward—that you are not progressive—that you are not a twentieth century merchant.

Look about you. Notice those who are successful—who are coming to the front—invariably they are the advertisers, who believe in the use of publications that get in touch with the people.

Don't lean too much on the factory in the matter of advertising.

It is true you want their help, and you are entitled to it up to a certain point, but do not make up your mind that you will only do as much advertising as they do. If you do that, you will be fooling yourself. Spend some of your own money, even if it is only a small amount.

The important thing is to establish your name. And to illustrate the point we are going to call you "John Smith."

You are being inquired about.

Some one asks: "What sort of man is John Smith? Is he the right sort of man to do business with? Does he live up to his word? Can he be depended upon? Does he give you a square deal?"

These questions are some of the reasons why you should advertise. Advertising will help you to establish yourself. People come to trust business men who advertise consistently.

Advertising is the surest way of establishing a reputation.

This is just the view-point you should take.

It isn't so much the car you handle—although that is important.

It is your own name and business that you should constantly seek to develop.

Money spent in consistent advertising always comes back to you in the form of increased business.

Don't hide yourself and then expect to be a leader in your business.

You cannot do it. How are people going to know about the superior value of the cars you handle unless you advertise?

The public deals with a man because it has confidence in him—because people are satisfied that he will keep his promises; this confidence, this high standard of business integrity can be built up only by proper methods and close attention to detail.

If you want to build up a successful business, you must build up this confidence—you must build up faith in yourself and in your organization. News spreads in an alarming way—automobile owners know each other, and if you are on the square the information spread by this "word of mouth" method will be of great help to you.

And so, money spent in advertising is never lost. Its power is sure. It does its work thoroughly—if given the opportunity.

Give your publicity a fair chance—do not expect the impossible of it just because you run one or two ads—but keep at it—that's what counts in advertising—and that's what brings "home the bacon."

You will find that the factories you do business with are more than willing to coöperate with you in the matter of advertising.

To begin with, they will gladly furnish you with a supply of all printed matter issued by them. In addition to this, they will provide you either free, or at a nominal cost, pennants, lantern slides, and novelties for distribution.

The advertising department of the factories you represent will be pleased to prepare for you a series of advertisements for your special use, and will furnish you with electrotypes for illustrating purposes.

Do not try to write your own advertisements or follow-up letters; nor any publicity work of any kind. Let a trained man do it for you. It isn't going to cost you a cent, so why not have it done correctly? Each factory you represent has an organized advertising department, or should have, and you should be able to secure at any time such advertisements as you wish for local use, news items for the newspapers in your territory and samples of any number of letters you may desire to use among prospects. Call upon the home advertising departments at any time. That's what they are there for (to assist the dealer) and they will gladly do anything for you within reason.

CHAPTER X

PROMOTION WORK

How fast are you moving with the business procession?

Do you "hustle" to the music of the day or does *your* band play "In the Shade of the Old Apple Tree"?

Are you an up-to-the-minute business man? Are you using all the modern business tools available?

Do you feel yourself growing each day? Does your place hum with progress and activity?

Do you appreciate what you are selling? Where do you stand in your town? Where does your line stand?

These are keen, competitive days. If you want to lead you must do as the leader does. You must keep close behind him. You must avail yourself of the opportunities of the day.

With each new day come new prospects. Do not forget it.

And you can never tell when a man is going to change his mind—that's why so many unexpected sales take place.

Here is another tip:

The best time to call on a man, for a final decision, is right after he has had his mid-day meal. As a rule, he is in fine fettle—at his best—and he is in better spirits than at any other time of the day—take advantage of it.

Make your strongest appeal then for he will listen to you patiently. Try it.

Do this: Pick out twenty-five, fifty or a hundred men in your town who have ample means, but who have never taken up the idea of buying a motor car. See them.

You might find them in a different frame of mind.

Do not forget a prospect—and do not let a prospect forget you.

Keep after him—but in the proper way, of course.

(1) After he has had his demonstration, mail him a copy of a strong testimonial letter you have from a local owner—preferably from a man he knows.

(2) After waiting two or three days, write him the first of a series of short letters. Your first one might be relative to the factory you represent, the care taken in manufacturing—you might also say something about the factory itself, the equipment, years in business, its ideals, etc.

(3) After a further lapse of two or three days, send him a note relative to your service and guarantee policy. This might be something along this line:

"Our interest in you does not cease when you purchase a car of us.

"No, indeed. We appreciate that to have a man satisfied is the best sort of an advertisement, for we are sure you would tell your friends how we are treating you.

"We are building up this business by

keeping our old friends and making new ones. Why not join our family of satisfied owners?"

It is now time to make a call, for you have made a certain mental impression and he should be in a mood to see you and talk business.

Your follow-up work is very important and you should not neglect it. Every piece of mail a prospect receives is certain to make a mental impression. You know how it is with yourself. You usually open and glance at every piece of mail you receive. So it is with prospects.

Do not depend on outside ideas all the time. Do a little thinking for yourself. Your ideas may be as good as those originated by others whom you are following.

Prospects—new prospects keep your business alive. Do not forget it. And you should have enough names on your lists to enable your men to keep busy all of the time. Lists may be compiled from tax rolls, business directories and automobile registrations.

CHAPTER XI

PRICES

Maintain prices. This attitude is quite likely to lose you some business in the beginning, but eventually it is sure to prove a valuable asset and strengthen you in the community in which you do business.

In addition to this, it will give the car, or cars, you may be selling a much better standing. The very fact that you will not take less than the list price will lead people to believe that you are handling a higher grade car than they had imagined. Prospective purchasers, even if they do not decide on your car, will have a better opinion, knowing that you believe the list price to be fair and that you are not willing and cannot sacrifice a cent of the money you ask.

The average man respects a price that the dealer will not lower.

To him it is the interpretation of full value. And in an unconscious way he will, the next time the opportunity presents itself, recommend your car on that account.

Cutting prices lowers the standard of your whole establishment. It cannot help but do that.

And again, you are legitimately entitled to your list price. It is fair, especially, in view of the fact that as a rule, it is necessary for you to make definite promises relative to service.

What would be your opinion of a business man and of his goods if he permitted you to purchase articles at your own terms and valuation? As a rule, cutting price does not mean an increase of business, so why practice it?

CHAPTER XII

DEMONSTRATIONS

It is safe to say that the average prospect, getting his trial spin in a demonstrating car, judges the stock model by its performance. And so you should see to it that every impression is a favorable one, and that you do not give him a single chance to entertain any doubt as to the ability of the car in question to do all the things and to perform in all the ways the average car is supposed to.

Notice the action of a prospect the next time you take him out to show him what the car will do. He approaches the car with his eyes scrutinizing it all over.

He notices, too, every move you make, with what ease you start the car—the get-a-way—the various speeds—hill-climbing ability—the way the car handles in crowded streets and every other minute thing.

And so, you must not only be on your guard, but you must have your demonstrator in such shape as to do everything creditably.

Perfect demonstrations are convincing and result in sales.

Poor demonstrations not only lose sales, but help, by word of mouth, to spread the information that your car was quite disappointing and so you should be positive that your demonstrating cars are perfect in every respect, all the time. Do not take a chance with a car that you know is not acting properly. And do not take an employee's word that it is, but try it yourself.

* * *

Benjamin B. Briscoe is of the opinion that a proper demonstration is of vital importance.

"The demonstrator is an important personage," he says, "or he should be, and only men who possess the combined qualifications of the salesman and the well-trained mechanic should be entrusted with the task of demonstrating a motor car to the prospective customer.

"The cases are legion in which the purchaser decided upon an automobile of another make simply because of the demonstrator's inability to present the good points of his car to advantage, with consequent injury to both dealer and purchaser; for the former had lost a sale, while the latter might have bought a better machine but for the poor impression created by an inefficient demonstrator.

"The most essential consideration in the make-up of the demonstrator is the aptness with which he seizes his opportunity. He makes his appointment with tact, and carefully avoids the exhibition of undue anxiety. If possible he chooses agreeable weather for the demonstration, and in case of rain or cold is careful to provide robes and coverings before starting on his trip.

"His car is kept scrupulously clean, as every car should be, and demonstrator and car show an atmosphere of ease that impresses the customer favorably. If the car is provided with a top, and fair weather attends the demonstration, the top should be folded back, for the occupant must be afforded a full and unobstructed view if he is to enjoy the ride.

"Our ideal demonstrator does not speed his car, unless he is requested to do so and when the road is clear, and then he handles his vehicle with care and with an unfailing precision that will indicate that controlling a motor vehicle is a simple thing. During the drive the future owner should be made acquainted with the purpose and operation of the different control levers, pedals, brakes, etc. Right here it is well to bear in mind the warning not to bewilder the novice with too many explanations at one time, for anything tending to confuse him is worse than no instruction at all. Special talking points should be enlarged upon and made to show their full value in an actual demonstration. Altogether it is safe to say that the demonstrator makes or unmakes the sale, since the customer to whom the car is demonstrated has very nearly reached the purchasing point.

"I have known dealers who, by proper attention, have maintained a demonstrating car in commission for two successive seasons, which is important on account of the fact that a demonstrating car should as much as possible have the appearance of a practically new car.

"Even with the best of operators some slight mishap is likely to occur. A tire will become punctured, for instance. I knew a demonstrator once who was exceedingly fond of profanity, and he would swear blue streaks at tires in general and tire makers in particular, with the result that whenever his demonstration was temporarily interrupted by a puncture, there would be no sale. His side partner, on the other hand, was a cheerful fellow, who would tackle a tire change gracefully, whistle a tune while making it, or maintain an animated conversation with the prospect. He even managed to turn the accident to advantage by suggesting to the prospect to step out of the car and watch him change the tire, mentioning casually that such a mishap might occur to him some day, and the sooner he knew all about it the better.

"A small investment made in a set of slip covers for the top hood not only saves the leather and top, but actually adds to the general appearance of the car.

"Too much care cannot be taken in keeping in constant touch with the prospect, for by neglecting him a few days the demonstrator permits his enthusiasm to cool off, and he may either become interested in some other car or lose his interest altogether."

CHAPTER XIII

THE GARAGE

We appreciate that this branch of the business is the hardest, and it is for this reason that you should give it due consideration.

See to it that your customers receive fair treatment from the men in charge of your garage.

If the garage is connected with your automobile selling agency, it is absolutely necessary that you conduct it with the aid of a man whom you can trust and who will prove helpful to you and your business. Choose for a foreman a man who is clean in his personal habits and will keep the garage, cars and stockroom in good order.

The selection of your garage crew is of vital importance, for it depends on the type of men who do your work as to whether you are going to keep customers satisfied.

Remember that your garage men come in contact with irritable customers.

Your men should treat everyone with courtesy and consideration.

They must not lose their tempers, for the average automobile purchaser thinks that this right belongs to him alone.

Order should be the most important point considered in connection with a garage.

Dirt is expensive and wasteful. Have a place for everything. Know at all times what you have on hand. Be systematic.

Do not hire cheap garage help. It will prove costly in the long run. Employ men who satisfy your foreman that they know their business. It will pay you, for they will be able to satisfy your customers. The garage division is as important as any other part of your business, if not more so. Do not forget it. Do not neglect it. Cultivate it. Watch it.

We know a man in New York, who has established a reputation for running the best garage in the metropolitan city. He employs forty men, and they are kept busy the whole year around. It was built up, first of all, by having a man in charge of the shop who had a thorough knowledge of automobile construction and was very conscientious in his work. He selected men who thought as he did, and the business that has been built up is truly remarkable, and proves conclusively what can be done if the proper methods are employed. We have been through that shop and have marveled at the cleanliness and order. It is a garage, but how different from the ordinary, dirty place one usually finds throughout the country.

Have order in the garage. Have the stock methodically and carefully arranged. And know what you have on hand. The way the average stockroom is kept, it is almost impossible to tell what stock is on hand.

Preach courtesy to your men in the garage. Tell them to guard their tongues in speaking with owners. Tell them to keep their temper. Tell them not to argue.

The garage part will either make or break your business. And your men have much to do with it.

You must be watchful of your service department. You should know what every division of this department costs you—know the amount of work done by each man each day (the money return value to you) and the amount of material used and for what particular job or jobs it was put into. You must be systematic, otherwise leaks will creep in and you will be behind in no time.

A good many dealers have no desire to make money in this department, they are quite satisfied if each month shows that it is breaking even, but there is never any occasion for a loss if you watch your men and material. The garage man who does not handle cars must make his business pay and there is no reason why the dealer should not. There are some dealers, many of them, whose garages show handsome profits.

CHAPTER XIV

SERVICE

You may think it easy to keep a customer, after you have made your initial sale, but you will often find it a most difficult thing.

In making your first sale, the customer was apparently impressed, and, providing the purchase was an automobile, the deal is not altogether closed as far as the buyer is concerned and he will be coming back to you time and time again.

It will be in these subsequent visits that he will judge you as to your method of treatment and the information he will give out to his acquaintances, who may be in the market for a car, will have effect on you. He is either going to say good things about you or that which is detrimental.

And so, for these reasons, it is absolutely

necessary to maintain a service policy that will be fair.

In other words, live up to your agreements and do not promise anything that you are not going to fulfill.

If you promise twelve months' service after the car is sold, keep that promise.

Do not let your promise be of an indefinite sort. Be honest with your customer and tell him the details of the guarantee. Do not promise anything you cannot afford to give. It will pay you to be frank in the beginning in order to avoid any future misunderstanding. The whole idea of your service policy should be such as to enable you to keep your customers and have them tell their friends of your fairness; in other words, become known as a man who "keeps his word." It's a most valuable asset to have and you are sure to profit by it.

Diplomacy of a high order is required in the automobile business. This is especially true in your relation with customers after sales have been made.

You must not forget that the individual buyer looks upon his purchase as one of the most important investments of his lifetime. Aside from purchasing a house, precious jewels, or something equally valuable, his motor car represents to him a lot of money. And in view of this fact, it is only natural that he should insist on your living up to the terms of the sale.

Diplomacy is required in handling customers who are temperamental and exacting in their demands. Make every effort to keep a friendly relationship with each customer. If he is unreasonable, appeal to his fairness. Cite a similar example in his own business. Show him how impossible it is to grant his request.

Every little while you find unreasonable purchasers and as a rule the dealer is to blame. And it all comes about because the car has not been sold on its merits.

The time is coming, and it is not far distant, when automobiles will be sold for what they are, as a piece of machinery, and not something mysterious that will go for ever; that you may abuse at will; that never requires attention; the parts of which never break; and other ridiculous popular notions. The whole after-trouble with prospects arises because of these reasons. And in addition to this, the average owner is never willing to blame himself or tell you he is at fault or when he is responsible for some mishap or other.

If you are sure a man is to blame, it will not do to tell him so, or argue with him, but rather to convince him by some method, that it is a charge he will have to pay, and give him good reason for it.

When a man makes an unreasonable request of you, he appreciates the unreasonableness of it as quickly, if not quicker, than you do and he is not going to hold a grudge against you if you tell him firmly that you cannot grant it.

You cannot afford to be lax in your dealings with owners who insist on taking advantage of you. They are not an asset to you and you are better off if they sever their business relations with you.

* * *

H. W. Slauson, in *Leslie's Weekly*, says: "Service is indeed a flexible word; it may range from the mere three months' or a year's guarantee on the part of the manufacturer to make good by replacement any part found to be defective in material or workmanship, to the view held by too many purchasers, which claims that service consists in the absolute promise on the part of the dealer to keep the car running under any and all conditions—entirely free of charge.

"Between these two views of what service should be, the dealer must choose his own course, always bearing in mind that his competitor may be offering enough more of 'free service' to make the rival car sold at what practically amounts to a cut price.

"Every car which leaves the factory of a reputable manufacturer is supposedly in perfect condition. But these adjustments, which are correct for the first hundred miles or so, may need to be changed after the machine is "worked in." In this case the dealer should be willing to make such adjustments for the purchaser without charge, provided the latter is so inexperienced that he cannot attend to this himself. Furthermore, the dealer should be ready and willing to accept for return to the factory such parts of the car as have been found to be defective in material or workmanship during the life of the manufacturer's guarantee.

"But there is a certain class of automobile buyers in this country who feel that, because they have favored a certain dealer and a certain company with their patronage, all connected with the organization are in duty bound to replace bearings if they have been burned out through lack of oil, to repair radiators damaged in collision, and, in short to keep the car in perfect condition, regardless of the fact that the owner's negligence forms the sole cause of its failure to prove satisfactory. It is the endeavor on the part of the dealer to satisfy this type of purchaser that constitutes one of the greatest dangers to the retail end of the automobile industry. The manufacturer is confronted with the danger of too much free service on the part of his retailers, which will eventually result in the bankruptcy of his best dealers; or in the lack of a fair and proper amount of service, which will result in a lack of prestige in territories in which this situation is most pronounced.

"Service is a word much used and abused by manufacturers and dealers. Enthusiastic salesmen are wont to promise more service than the companies they represent could in all fairness afford to give. But the manufacturer of the modern car is really morally required to give but very little free service. The service that he and his dealers render should represent a legitimate charge, always bearing in mind, of course, the exceptions that might be included under the manufacturer's guarantee. But service is as much the ability to make repairs and replacements as it is the free disposition of valuable time on the car. We hear much of service stations of the large automobile companies being built in the leading cities of the country. The purchaser of the car in a small town feels that his brother in the large city has the advantage in his accessibility to one of these large service stations, but, contrary to the popular impression, most of these service stations are self-supporting. There is but little free service rendered there. They are merely large garage and repair shops run in connection with the dealer controlling that territory. Their work is specialized and is generally restricted to repairs on one particular make of car. Work is charged for at usual rates, but it is naturally expected that it will be more efficiently performed where each mechanic is thoroughly familiar with the construction of the car made by the manufacturer maintaining these service stations.

"The purchaser of a car from a duly accredited representative in a small town can receive equally efficient free service in so far as that relates to adjustment of the car and the offering of expert advice as to its care and operation. Any service other than this he should expect to pay for, whether the work be done in a large service station of a distributing center, or in a local garage—providing, of course, that the car lives up to its guarantee.

"There is only one common ground on which manufacturer, dealer and purchaser can meet in a discussion of service, and that is the courteous willingness of the first two to make the last-named a satisfied customer within reasonable limits. Willingness to adjust a carburetor, courtesy in offering advice as to the cleaning of the motor, and a complete knowledge of the car and its requirements on the part of the dealer, form a more perfect service combination than can the largest and best-equipped service station in the hands of a dealer whose motto is 'The Customer is Never Right.'"

* * *

Elmer Apperson, President of Apperson Brothers Automobile Company, anent this question, says:

"A manufacturer should keep to the letter of his guarantee and the dealer, in turn, should keep all promises made to the individual purchaser. Manufacturers may have different opinions as to what constitutes ideal service, but whatever it is, it should be understood by all concerned. The purchaser has every right to know what he is to expect.

"With a full understanding of what the purchaser is to receive without charge, and what he is to pay for, there will never be any reason for argument.

"The manufacturer who is a permanent factor in the industry is anxious to keep the good will of his customers and he is only too willing to do anything consistent with good business judgment. The manufacturer not only wants to keep his customers, but is anxious to add to his list of followers and wants the public to know him as a 'fair and square' business man.

"Some dealers consider a certain period of free service a good investment for them in retaining the good-will of their customers.

"In the matter of adjustments, the dealer should consider himself not in the light of a purchaser from the automobile manufacturer, but as his representative. Most manufacturers will allow credit on defective parts (and an occasional defect will develop even in the best of cars) only after they have tested it for defects. And they have special tests to discover flaws, which are fair to all concerned.

"Therefore in this matter the dealer should accept the decision of the manufacturer. His task is a delicate one, it is admitted, but tact is one of the requirements in the make-up of the successful dealer."

CHAPTER XV

GARAGE AND ACCESSORIES

The modern garage man is a business man. The physician or lawyer or real estate man would make a poor job rebuilding a motor.

The garage man whose trend is entirely mechanical cannot hope to be successful.

He may be a skilled mechanic; he may supervise all of the work that is turned out; or he may do a good share of it himself. All of his work may be of the highest grade; his customers may be perfectly satisfied; and he may enjoy a steady trade. But still he will not succeed.

For he has not learned good business practice. He is not a business man.

He may make money, but if he does, it is simply because he is a good guesser; for he does not know when he is making money.

Your business man-garage man does know. He knows just what divisions of his business are paying. He knows just what accessory does not yield a reasonable profit. He knows just what workman is costing him the most money—very seldom the highest paid man.

The garage man with his nose in the motor loses perspective. He cannot see beyond the spring he is repairing or the valve he is grinding and the amount he is to receive for it.

He should step back and look his business over in an impersonal way, and he will find that he, himself, is the most wasteful man in his shop. For he is wasting his time on petty things.

A successful garage must have business methods. If the business warrants it, a good bookkeeper should be employed.

If the business is too small to warrant this expenditure, the garage owner should designate himself business manager for certain regular periods.

He should then analyze his business, pick it to pieces and see what makes it go. And even should a bookkeeper be employed, the garage owner should have the ability to get the full significance of his figures.

Do not think that a lack of bookkeeping knowledge presages disaster. It is not necessary that you be a bookkeeper. There are few successful business men who would recognize a set of books if they saw them.

Business sense and bookkeeping are not synonymous.

Business sense means knowledge of your business.

Business sense is knowing where you are making money and where you are losing it—where your efforts should be concentrated and where the business needs doctoring—building up.

You may be enjoying a fair profit on your repair work and losing on your stock of accessories. The average of the profits on one and the losses of the other may show a slight profit. But how much greater your returns, if both your repair work and accessory stock were paying. And without business acumen you are groping in the dark, for no one will point out your mistakes to you—your employees cannot do it, neither can your customers.

The remedy for this condition is, in a broad term, organization. Or to be more specific, system.

For instance, in the handling of accessories it is not the store with the greatest stock that does the largest business. It is usually the store with the most frequent turn-over; that is, the establishment that sells its entire stock of each article carried the greatest number of times in a year.

Of course, a stock must be varied and in this sense should be large. But the store that turns over its entire stock three or four times a year and buys in minimum quantities is the most successful; advocates of large stocks with quantity discounts, to the contrary notwithstanding. This holds true of any business.

It follows, therefore, that a system must be installed to meet the necessity for accurate information on this subject. This does not necessarily mean that such a system must be elaborate. For too much system will eventually develop a giant that will menace any business.

The name of this giant is overhead expense. This must be kept down within reason.

The garage owner will undoubtedly devise certain methods of his own which will answer his purpose. It is only necessary to keep a careful check upon purchases, stock on hand and returns.

For this purpose a simple card record will prove of value.

One card should be used for each item carried in stock with spaces for the recording of date of purchase, amount, quantity on hand and quantity disbursed. Provision should also be made for recording sources of supply, brief description of article, cost, discount, selling price, etc. The following sample card form will suggest the method to be followed:

Name_____ Description_____ Cost_____ Discount_____ Selling price_____			RECEIVED		DISBURSED		Balance
Date	Purchased from	Amount	Date	Amount	Date	Amount	Total	

FORM 3

By this method, you have at your fingers' ends accurate knowledge of the movement of your stock.

Do not buy heavily. Do not let old stock accumulate. If you are "stuck" with any one item, cut the price and use it as a special to draw trade. Better to give it away and get rid of it than have it occupy valuable space on your shelves.

In passing, keep your shelves and stock clean—orderly—and inviting. Your customers will appreciate it and it will save you much time and trouble.

What is true of accessories is also true of automobile parts and even to a greater extent is it necessary to be in possession of complete knowledge. For automobile parts are, in a measure, seasonable. And while it would appear that they are a permanent commodity in truth, a part soon becomes theoretically dead. There is nothing more useless than an automobile part with no market for it.

With parts it is possible and advisable to

maintain a record of each disbursement. This should be done with the exception only of those parts whose cost is insignificant.

The garage man usually has a selling connection with one or more automobile manufacturers. If this is not the case, you will find as a rule that it is more profitable to specialize in one or two makes. Those makes for which you are best equipped to handle the repair work.

All manufacturers designate symbol numbers to the various parts of their respective automobiles. Each part, no matter how small, is known and referred to by number.

In handling your stock, use their numbers as far as practicable. Your customers will purchase by the manufacturer's number and you, in turn, will order by this number, so it will be a saving of time to handle your stock and records by this system.

Keep your parts in bins accordingly. Keep your bins numbered. Keep your bins clean and orderly. Do not mix parts for various makes of cars.

The same principle of quick turn-over applies to parts as well as accessories, and your record should be kept in much the same way, except, as before stated, it is wise to record each individual disbursement.

A stock record card should bear, as well as the name of the part, its corresponding part number. They should be filed according to number and should also give the location of the bin containing the parts. Should a customer order by description of the part for his car, the number can readily be obtained by referring to the manufacturer's parts book. These should, of course, be kept on hand at all times.

The cut on next page is a sample form for a parts record card.

A loose leaf sheet may be used, if desired, and it has the added advantage that it may be kept in a binder. Cards must be taken from the index box or drawer to record the necessary entry. In returning them they are very apt to be placed in the wrong position. A loose leaf sheet is not removed

| Part Name _____ Part No. _____ |
| Specifications _____ Section _____ |
| Max. _____ Min. _____ Used on Models _____ Bin _____ Years _____ |
| Size _____ Cost _____ List _____ Discount _____ |

Date	Received	Quantity	Total	Date	Requisition Number	Quantity Disbursed	Date	Balance

FORM 4

from its binder for entries and therefore cannot be lost or misplaced.

In the reproduction, Form 5, of a loose leaf sheet of this type, the first four columns form a record of goods ordered; the next four, goods received; the next eight, two sets of four columns each, disbursements; and the last six, three sets of two columns each, show amount on hand.

This record automatically checks the accuracy of your figures—the cumulative totals must balance. The cumulative total of amount ordered must equal total received unless there are still goods to be received on the order. Should you receive an over-shipment, record in the order columns in red ink adding amount of over-shipment to cumulative total, and for order number inserting "O. S." Handle short shipment in the same manner, subtracting amount from cumulative total. If material is scrapped or destroyed subtract from the columns, entering in red ink.

Each disbursement must be listed in dis-

FORM 5

bursed column and added to cumulative total in these columns; also in balance column and subtracted from balance. The sum of the cumulative total disbursements and balance on hand must equal amount received, which, in turn, must balance the amount ordered.

Inventories should be entered in red ink in disbursed and balance columns. Should you inventory fewer parts than the balance total, enter in red ink under reference "adjustment"; add the difference between inventory figure and balance figure to disbursement total; subtract from balance; then enter the inventory figures and the sheet will balance.

If your business is too small to warrant the expense of printing forms as elaborate as those illustrated, do not dispense with a record altogether. A plain inexpensive index card, three by five inches or four by six inches, will answer the purpose of a record of purchases, cost, names, part numbers, etc. And provision should also be made for the entry of inventories, which should be taken often. This will not prove burdensome to a small business.

It is not suggested that these records be kept by yourself. They are simple enough for your employees to understand and keep up without a great amount of time being spent upon them.

You should, however, be conversant with them and see that they are correctly kept. If the information you gain from them is incorrect they are worse than no record at all.

The sample forms presented are not intended to be arbitrary, but may be changed as local conditions require. These are matters which should have the attention of the garage owner or manager just as much as the placing of stocks or hiring of men.

CHAPTER XVI

GARAGE AND REPAIRS

The most difficult part of the garage business, both in its actual accomplishment and in making it profitable, is the repair work—the actual work which consumes the time of your employees.

This, of course, should be done carefully, accurately and speedily. A man with his car out of commission is always in a rush. It is perfectly natural. You, in his position, would exhibit no greater degree of patience.

And he will always believe that your charges are extortionate. The average car owner acts upon the theory that all repair men are in a league for the sole purpose of robbing him.

In a measure he is not to be censured for this attitude, for he has been wrongly educated. Almost from the inception of the automobile business, the salesman, in his eagerness for immediate sales, has made all manner of extravagant claims for the car he represents.

An ideal service system has been pictured to the purchaser as maintained solely for his benefit and—"If anything goes wrong with the car, Mr. Buyer, come in any time and we will make it good."

The buyer has not forgotten these promises, and he has forced the salesman or garage owner to keep his word—or the reputation of his car suffers. And many a once-thriving business has gone to the wall for this single reason.

The purchaser has been led to expect too much from his motor car. For fear of losing a sale, the salesman has neglected to tell him that he has bought a piece of machinery that requires care and attention. The general impression that he has received is that an automobile is a species of perpetual motion, provided a little gasoline is poured in now and then and, of course, an occasional tire replaced. And then with his car neglected until some serious damage has resulted, he heaps curses upon the head of the blameless manufacturer and loudly claims his due of service from the firm who sold him the car.

It is this much-abused term "service" that is the reef upon which many a ship of successful business has foundered. And it is a hard matter to mark just the channel which guides to safety from too much so-called service and to the safe harbor of good-will gained by a proper amount of policy work.

The line must be drawn and it must not be too flexible. The purchaser of a car is undoubtedly entitled to some consideration in this respect. Minor adjustments, which do not entail too much time, or expense, should be performed gratuitously, and such courtesies will redound to your benefit.

But replacements and repairs, which the manufacturer will not make good under his guarantee, should not be performed by the dealer.

You will find that factories are very strict in this respect. They hold to the very letter of their guarantee, which is worded necessarily for their protection. And their policy allowance is kept within very close bounds. This is because the factory is run upon a business basis and an endeavor is made to educate the owner to a proper respect for the mechanism of his machine. It is an invariable rule that the more strict a manufacturer is in this respect, the greater his business and the higher the standing of his car.

The garage owner should make the most of this example and his "No" should mean "No."

There are exceptions to all rules and this complex matter of service will require judgment and tact. This, of course, applies more specifically to the dealer—the salesman-garage owner.

But the individual repair man suffers also, for upon his returns for repair work is dependent his livelihood. And it rankles the car owner to have to pay for seemingly insignificant adjustments, which he has been accustomed to receive without charge from his dealer.

He, too, will find it necessary to exercise discretion in the service he gives, or his policy allowance will administer a "knock-out" to his profits.

The dealer can, and often does, maintain a garage and repair shop simply as an accommodation for his customers and is perfectly satisfied if he breaks even, for he depends on his sales of cars to make his money. But the repair man cannot just "break even" and continue in business. He must operate at a profit.

In either case, it calls for a nice calculation of costs and returns, with the ever-varying human element playing a leading rôle. For the time consumed on a job enters into every transaction.

For this reason complete records of every transaction are absolutely essential. Not only for the purpose of computing your charge correctly, but for future reference in case of disputes.

Where a number of men are employed, time slips cannot be dispensed with, although clocks and a complicated time-keeping system are not necessary. Requisitions should also be provided for obtaining parts from stock in order that stock records may be kept clear. By numbering these consecutively, or according to job numbers, and entering this number on the stock record card, you are supplied with a double check upon all the parts used for repairs.

Some sort of repair order form, which carries complete information of each individual job, and from which the invoice is made out, should also be used.

When the volume of business admits, an ideal form for this purpose is made up of a sheet, a card and an envelope—the sheet is an itemized list of the work done and parts used; the card to be attached to the job and the envelope to show a summary of the work and costs; to contain all requi-

FORM 6

sitions and time tickets and to be filed in the office.

By referring to Form 6 you will notice that the first sheet, in addition to giving the name and address of the car owner, description of the car, date job is received and approximate date promised, also constitutes an order by the car owner to do the work and furnish material. Provision is also made for a record of the delivery of the completed job. This is a full release by the owner. The last four columns are filled in from the workmen's time tickets.

The reverse of this sheet, Form 6A, lists all of the material used, giving cost and requisition number. Any work which you are not equipped to handle and which is done outside is listed at the bottom of the sheet and total amount of charge is computed. This is not meant to be an invoice, but is an internal record to be retained by your bookkeeper or accountant. The invoice is made out from this sheet.

Part of the card, Form 6B, registers with

FORM 6A

FORM 6B

Car _____	ORDER NO. 3260
Model ____ Car No. _____	Owner _____
License No. _____	Address _____
Date _____ 191__	

The original Repair Order and all Requisitions for Material and Workman's Time Slips and any other papers connected with this Job are to be filed in this Envelope

COST RECORDS

Labor Cost						Returns		
Workman	Regular Time		Over Time		Amount	Cash Received	
	Hours	Rate	Hours	Rate				
						Cash Sale No.		
						Invoice No.		
						Charge Acct		
						Invoice No.		
						Policy Allowance		
						Total Proceeds		
Cost of Labor								
Cost of Material						Total Amount of Job per Repair order	
Cost of Outside Work						Collection made by	
Total Cost								

This envelope to be filed under name of customer alphabetically

FORM 6C

the first sheet and is made out simply by using a sheet of carbon paper. This card is the workman's instructions to make the repairs. It is hung on the job and is not removed until the customer has signed the release on the face of the first sheet. Space is also provided for a check-up of the equipment of the car. This is a valuable precaution. This card is filed in the repair shop when the job is completed and is your foreman's permanent record.

The envelope, Form 6C, as before stated, is a summary and cost record for office use and is convenient for filing all of the records pertaining to the job. This is not absolutely necessary, as the time slips and requisitions may be clipped to the original repair order and filed in this manner.

It will be noted that the forms are numbered in triplicate. The envelope containing the original order (or the repair order alone) is filed alphabetically under the customer's name in the office. The card of instructions for the workman is filed in the repair shop numerically, thus providing a cross reference.

Form 7 is a time slip to be used in connection with the repair order, forming the basis for the time charge and also for the pay-roll. The method of its use is self-evident. After these slips have served their purpose, they are filed in the envelope or with the repair order.

A material requisition for this system is shown in Form 8. It is numbered in duplicate, one copy being retained by the stock-keeper, and the other going to the bookkeeper for recording and filing with the time tickets.

From these requisitions stock record entries are made on the stock record card shown on page 129.

Of course a much more simple system may be used, and this is advisable if only a few jobs are handled a day, the following method suiting the smaller business:

Form 9 is a tag or card which constitutes the repair order on the back of which (Form 10) time and parts cost are totaled by the

```
┌─────────────────────────────────────┐
│      INDIVIDUAL  TIME  SLIP.        │
│ Fill out one slip for each item on Repair Order │
│ and individual slip for each day on that Work   │
├─────────────────────────────────────┤
│ Workman No. _____ Job No._____│
│ Customer    _____ │
│ Work to be done _____ │
│                                     │
├─────────────────────────────────────┤
│ Hours  │                            │
│ Worked │                            │
│ Start    Stop      Start    Stop    │
│                                     │
│                                     │
│        ─────────────────────────    │
│              Signature of Workman   │
└─────────────────────────────────────┘
```

FORM 7

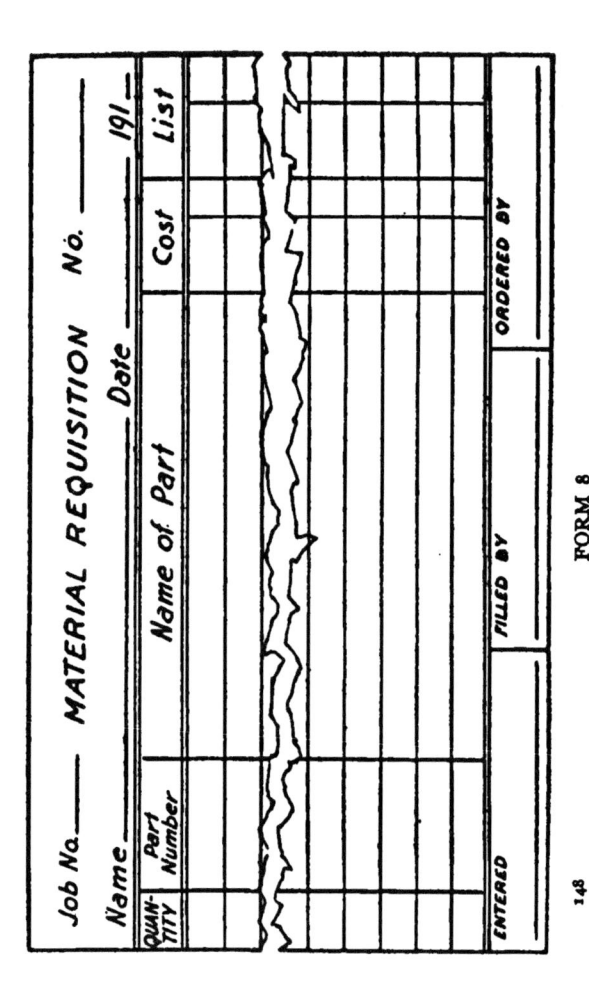

FORM 8

BOSTON GARAGE COMPANY
Repair Tag

Date _____ 191__

Name _____

Address _____

Promised _____

Repairs Required

FORM 9

FORM 10

bookkeeper when job is completed. Time slips and requisitions are of course used in the same manner as outlined previously, although still simpler forms may also be used for these if desired.

Forms 11 and 11A show a card a little more elaborate than Form 9, but not so detailed as Form 6. After the foregoing explanation this card should be self-explanatory.

Gasoline and oil should be handled in the same manner as the stock. A considerable sum of money may be lost by loose methods in handling these two items. No gasoline should be given out except by written order. Various methods of checking this will suggest themselves to the garage owner.

Many garages have found it profitable to maintain a complete card index of their customers, listing thereon various information about their cars and, of course, noting also all work done. This is an idea borrowed from the modern physician, who keeps a record of his patients in this manner.

BOSTON GARAGE CO. **REPAIR ORDER** ORDER NO. 3260

Date _____ 191__

This is your authority to do the work listed below and
to supply the materials necessary to effect the repairs

Car No. _____ Model _____

When Promised _____

Signed _____

Address _____ Deliver to _____

INSTRUCTIONS

Have examined the Charges shown on the back of this sheet amounting to _____ and find them correct

Signed _____

Customer

Invoiced _____ Invoice No. _____ Date Completed _____ 191__

Delivered by _____ Date Delivered _____ 191__

FORM 11

FORM 11A

However, as it entails quite an amount of additional work, and is not absolutely essential, its use is open to question unless a complete record is desired.

Careful records along these lines, will keep bookkeeping down to a minimum.

Run your business on a cash basis.

The fewer accounts you open, the less bookkeeping you will have to do. The less bookkeeping, the lower the overhead expense. The lower the overhead expense the greater the profits.

Then, too, by following this method you do away with all collection expense, and in the long run you will hold your customers better.

It will undoubtedly be necessary to open some accounts as you will have regular storage accounts and some monthly service accounts.

But in your ordinary business, get cash.

CHAPTER XVII

SECOND-HAND CARS

The second-hand problem is the bane of the automobile business. Carelessness and lack of judgment in second-hand matters have caused the ruin of more than one dealer. So the beginner in the business should approach this subject with great caution. You cannot be too careful. You cannot be too skeptical about your own judgment in the matter. Take the position of a most impartial judge. And do not be influenced in the slightest degree by what the second-hand owner says. He is the seller in this case, even if he is trying to make a trade deal, so it is well to discount most of the claims.

Play safe. It is much better to place an undervalue on a second-hand car than to overrate it. Be as certain as it is possible to be of its cash value, for you should see to it that the new car represents list price in *cash* and should not, in part, be represented by an inflated value placed on a second-hand car. You are in business to make money and not for the purpose of meeting the demands of car owners who place ridiculous prices on their machines when they are ready to make a trade for new ones.

Always allow, or rather deduct, from your valuation a sum sufficient to cover the cost of overhauling the car you are taking in. For in nine cases out of ten it will need it and it is a wise precautionary measure. However, do not expend too much time on this sort of work.

Your business is selling new cars, not buying old ones. And if you take second-hand cars in, be sure that the cost does not cut into the profit you were originally entitled to.

Do not allow second-hand cars to accumulate. See to it that your salesmen are informed as quickly as possible, so they may be able to find a purchaser. It is also a good rule to place the responsibility of selling each second-hand car on the man taking it in as part payment on a new car.

Do not underrate the man who buys a second-hand car. He is your customer and should be treated as such.

The man who buys a second-hand car today is your prospect for a new model tomorrow, and if you have given him a square deal on the first transaction, your way is already paved to an easy sale. For he is your friend.

When he is in your showroom or garage examining the second-hand model, do not overlook the opportunity to point out the superior features of your regular line. It is time well invested.

And do not forget him. Place his name upon your prospect list and call upon him occasionally. Keep in touch with him by mailing him a folder or circular from time to time. Do not let him forget you.

In moving used cars, liner advertisements will be found to be of valuable assistance.

In wording these advertisements, do not misrepresent the value of the car. For while you may get a greater number of inquiries, in the end you will have acquired an enemy in the purchaser, instead of making a friend.

It is also well to keep prominently displayed, either in your windows or elsewhere, a card or sign listing the used cars you have on hand and their prices.

CHAPTER XVIII

THE COMMERCIAL CAR

There is no use denying the fact that the commercial car business has not kept pace with the pleasure car division. This is true both from a mechanical standpoint and as a matter of interest on the part of those who would be benefited by the adoption of trucks.

There are many reasons why business interests have been backward. The most important one of all is probably the fact that, in the beginning, commercial vehicles were not mechanically sound. They were either too heavy or too light and the majority of them were cast aside shortly after being put in use.

But all this has changed, for in the past five years much hard work has been done by designers, engineers and others interested in the work.

And, today, there are many reliable trucks on the market which are used in every business imaginable. Today commerical cars deliver everything from an angel cake to a load of structural steel. Trucks are made in all sizes and capacities.

Should you handle a line of trucks?

It all depends on the location and territory covered by your business.

If, after a careful investigation, you are satisfied that they can be sold in your territory, you may enter into negotiations with reliable factories making commercial vehicles suitable for the business establishments located in your districts.

But be careful. Do not select an untried truck. Do not take any chances with anything in the experimental stage. You cannot afford to do it. You can lose money too fast in this end of the business.

There is money to be made in this field, providing the territory warrants it. It all depends on what your territory is able to absorb in the commercial line.

* * *

"The dealer has not yet realized the possibilities of the commercial car," says W. L. Day, Vice-President of the General Motors Truck Company.

"Naturally, the first people to buy motor trucks were the 'big concerns;' those who had large quantities of merchandise to move.

"Almost invariably such concerns bought heavy duty trucks and few of the early manufacturers of motor trucks thought of catering to the lighter field.

"Many dealers today, when they think of motor trucks, think only of the heavy car and do not realize that there is a big field for the sale of motor trucks outside of the large centers and among people who have no need for a fleet of trucks.

"The day is rapidly approaching when the well-to-do farmer, and especially the dairy farmer and the truck gardener will use motor trucks.

"In selecting a line of trucks the dealer should choose a line that will enable him to compete for not only the heavy, but the light trade of his locality. He should study conditions and be able to recommend the right truck for his customer's business, for it is a fact that many prospective purchasers of motor trucks do not know what they ought to buy and are frequently persuaded to buy a truck that is either too heavy or too light for their work.

"To sell a man a truck that is not adapted to his requirements means a dissatisfied customer and creates a 'knocker' in the community against motor trucks.

"On the other hand, if the dealer is in position to recommend and furnish the *right* truck, the customer is pleased and becomes a valuable assistant in promoting the motor truck trade of that locality."

* * *

"Through the past ten years—more particularly the last five years," says M. L. Pulcher, Vice-President and General Manager of the

Federal Motor Truck Company, "I have seen the motor truck industry lift itself out of a veritable 'Slough of Despond,' out of a mire of discouraging conditions, up on to a clean, solid footing, the stability of which might well be envied by many other industries.

"One of the most difficult and thoroughly discouraging features of this industry has been that of getting dealers,—good live dealers who know where the business is and how to get it.

"The average automobile dealer, providing he has a pretty fair line of pleasure cars, can make money more easily by pushing their sale than by pushing the sale of motor trucks —consequently he usually neglects his motor truck account in favor of his pleasure car accounts. Most dealers in motor trucks alone, have in the past been only mildly successful. A few who have worked exceptionally hard along the right lines, have been very successful with trucks alone.

"We feel certain, however, that these conditions have been eliminated to a large extent. Years ago the dealer was up against a pretty hard proposition. The average motor truck was not what it should have been and all the profits a dealer made, and more, would be eaten up by free service which the dealer had to give purchasers. The dealer has been educated away from the free service policy and the unscrupulous manufacturer has been forced, by competition, either to drop out in a hurry before damage is done, or bring his product up to a certain standard.

"The dealer should, we believe, concentrate upon a small territory, rather than try to handle too large an area. Such concentration brings more in the end than more widely scattered efforts will, for, in a comparatively small territory the dealer can tell from actual observation of the requirements of the various businesses, whether one-ton or five-ton trucks would be more efficient—in other words, he can get a better focus on the demand and how best to supply it. Bad mistakes have been made in the past through dealers not having studied their territory's requirements, and because, handling the wrong capacities and having to sell them, they 'force' the purchaser, who is then disappointed to find results are not what were to be expected. The wrong size trucks can't get the right kind of results.

"Through concentration on a small territory the securing of new, live prospects, and the following up of those prospects, is made easier and much more effective.

"One of the best ways I know of to secure the immediate, and, in a large percentage of cases, the permanent interest of prospects, is to write them personal letters after close observation of their transportation equipment. Whenever horses are seen laboring under hard conditions fatigued by heat, stuck in the snow, fallen on slippery roads,— that is the time to show the user of those horses the inefficiency, the wanton waste and the cruelty of such haulage methods. Backing up leads of that sort with literature produced especially for the line of work the prospect is in, and with exact figures showing cost of operation with trucks *versus* horses, will nine times out of ten start the prospect in the direction you want him. There is no end to the interesting savings and advantages that should be brought to the attention of the prospect—information that should be handled diplomatically, however, and followed up regularly until the time for demonstrating the trucks themselves—after which should come the sale.

"At proper intervals between personal letters, direct mail advertising, etc., should come personal interviews by the salesman, and the salesman who has facts and figures to show can usually get a very interested interview with the men who buy trucks.

"Telling the man what trucks are doing in his line of business, then applying that information to show what they could do for him, and telling him what he can save over his present equipment are the essentials—above all else—in following up prospects, whether it be through advertising literature or personal contact. The mechanical features of the truck enter into the final stages of the selling, and should not, in my opinion, be sprung too early on the prospect.

"Every concern with a good rating in Dun's and Bradstreet's, and which requires transportation equipment of any kind, can use some kind of motor truck to better advantage than any other equipment now known. These concerns are the prospects. Get them by advertising—good advertising, that is made as close to the prospect's business as possible.

"There will be, conservatively estimating, more than a billion and a quarter of dollars spent for commercial cars in the next ten years by American business men alone, such is the magnitude of this industry after a comparatively few years of development."

CHAPTER XIX

ELECTRIC VEHICLES

The electric vehicle has a definite place in the automobile world, but it has little in common with gasoline cars.

Although serviceable and dependable, the electric has not yet reached its highest development. At the present its field of operation is limited almost entirely to city traffic. This is due to the fact that it cannot operate far from its base or charging station.

Storage batteries are heavy. And until they can be lightened and made more efficient, the electric vehicle will be inferior to the gasoline propelled car. This is only a matter of time, for some of the best minds in the country are engaged in solving the problem of the electric.

At the present stage of its development,

the electric as a pleasure car is a woman's car—it is almost exclusively society's vehicle. It is not adapted to country use and its simple control makes it admirably suited for women.

The dealer for an electric must maintain a garage and equipment to recharge batteries. It is not very feasible to combine in a garage the handling of gasoline motor cars and electrics. The dealer in electrics usually handles electrics exclusively.

It is, of course, necessary that the salesman or dealer be located in a city—small towns cannot support a trade. It is also necessary for the salesman to handle his proposition in an entirely different manner from that followed in handling gasoline cars.

If the salesman of the latter should be neat and clean in his dress, the man endeavoring to sell electrics should be fastidious in his attire. He must be capable of meeting society on society's own terms.

The same principles of salesmanship apply here. But you should remember that the electric is even more a pleasure car than the gasoline type. A woman is more interested in the cushions, lights, upholstery and finish than she is in the motor. Practically all electric cars are inclosed cars and these points should be played up well.

There is money to be made in electrics, but it requires salesmanship of a high order and an unlimited amount of patience and tact.

Refer to Chapter XX, "The Car and the Woman." The points brought out in this chapter apply with even greater force to the man who is selling electrics.

To the woman prospect, lay particular stress upon quietness, ease of control, cleanliness and elegance. With the physician and business man, feature the fact that an electric requires little attention, its low up-keep cost, dependability and greater convenience where many stops are made.

* * *

Electric delivery vehicles and trucks are giving very satisfactory service. The electric is well adapted to this purpose. It is not called upon to cover great distances and make long tours. Neither is great speed essential.

The truck is a utility and must be sold as a utility. Keep this thought uppermost. Dollars-and-cents facts are what the business man wants to know.

The truck salesman must be not only a commercial car salesman, but a business analyst. Every one wants a pleasure car with varying degrees of desire. The average business man does not want a truck. He believes he is doing well enough without it or he would not be in business.

Your task then is to convince him that a commercial car is necessary to his business. To do this you must know his business. You must make a study of it. He must be shown facts about his own affairs.

You cannot convince a florist that he needs your commercial car by citing a furniture man's requirements.

Therefore, know your prospect. Know his business. Know some features of it better than he, himself, does.

Show him where his investment will return a definite profit to him. Show him how he can afford this unusual, to him, expenditure. Show him how it will increase his business.

First, sell him commercial car service. Then sell him your particular make of car.

You ought to know, better than he, just what style of truck is adapted to his purpose and you should sell him that style.

Most truck manufacturers furnish trucks of varying capacities and usually the salesman is in a better position to advise his customer as to his requirements than the customer is himself.

Electric and gasoline commercial vehicles cover much the same field and the choice of one over the other will be governed almost entirely by local conditions.

Do not try to sell a man a truck which does not suit his purpose. It is as fatal to future business as is deliberate misrepresentation of any product.

Remember you are dealing with a business

man. Talk to him on a business basis. Be brief but explicit.

Statistical letters which are pithy will have a good effect. Do not send out long letters and hope to have them read.

Make your calls brief. Drive home a new thought each time you call.

* * *

The same rules apply to the electric garage as to the gasoline car garage, except that there should be a much greater amount of garaging.

Service should be of the highest order, for a satisfied customer means a steady, definite income.

Likewise cleanliness should be carried to an extreme.

It is hardly practicable to attempt to establish the electric garage upon a cash basis. Most of your customers will garage their cars and depend upon you for all necessary repairs. Upon this basis a regular monthly charge, including charging, repairing, garaging, washing, etc., will be found feasible.

However, this should be calculated to a

nicety as it is very easy to be taken advantage of by the owner who feels that he is entitled to be careless.

It should hardly be necessary to state that your men should be competent electricians. The same principles of the gasoline garage cost system will apply to the electric, although, of course, special forms must be devised to suit the different conditions.

CHAPTER XX

THE CAR AND THE WOMAN

Don't forget the "woman in the case."

Play to her vanity and prove to her that the car you are trying to sell is especially adapted to her use.

You have probably realized yourself that you have to convince the "lady of the house" as much as you do the man who pays the bills.

She has so much to say in the actual closing of a sale, that the clever salesman does not neglect her a minute. It is well to treat her with consideration by giving her as much of the sales talk as you do the man.

And be sure and point out to her the important things in which she is interested.

You should tell her that owing to the simplicity of the starting system, she would be able to drive the car, and on account of its safety features and dependability, she could, if she wished, make quite a trip by herself.

You should point out to her the comfortable riding qualities—the stylish body—and the popularity of the color scheme.

Above all, if you wish to appeal to her especially, tell her the car you sell has marked individuality.

Yes, indeed, consider the woman every time; for if you should be fortunate enough to secure her interest, you will have made great progress toward a sale.

There are more women drivers than ever before, not only that, but they are purchasers of gasoline cars, so they enter into the business more than the average man imagines.

Always make it a point to show her details —the attractive little things that are dear to a woman's heart.

If you are trying to sell her husband a closed car, you cannot be too painstaking in convincing her of the many details possessed by the car in question. Point out the curtains, vanity boxes, cut-glass fixtures, comfort, beauty; in fact, do not let a single item escape her.

CHAPTER XXI

THE BOY OF TODAY

The boy of today is the automobile purchaser of tomorrow—and is a power now.

Don't neglect him—when he asks questions—inform him—be nice to him—treat him like a "grown-up"—he is going to be one soon.

It is surprising the automobile knowledge that is stored in the average boy's head. He knows all about cars—especially if his father owns one, but even if he doesn't, the boy is keeping posted.

And when his father is ready to buy—the boy has his little say—and sometimes—yes, quite often, — the son has the deciding word.

So, "get next" to the boy in the family; when he comes into your salesroom treat him with the same courtesy you would bestow on the man with a check in his hand.

His opinion might count—you don't know how soon—so win him over to you.

And then again, the average boy drives. The average boy knows more about a car than his father does. The average boy picks up information on the street. And doesn't he watch each car as it glides by? He is vitally interested. And did you ever count the boys at motor shows and what great catalog collectors they were? It is true that each boy does not represent purchasing power (through his parents) but you do not know how soon he will, and for these reasons he should not be treated as a nuisance. In a good many cases he is not given any attention at all although he is entitled to it.

CHAPTER XXII

YOU—AND YOUR OPPORTUNITIES

Emerson said "An institution is the lengthened shadow of one man."

Your business, its appearance, the men under you, their method of work, their energy, their enthusiasm—all this reflects your personality, your energy, your business and your method of work.

Your organization will be just what you make it. It might be a big and strong one, or, it might be small and weak—all depending on "the lengthened shadow of one man."

You, as the boss, are the biggest man in your organization. Don't forget it.

Make your personality count. Put yourself in the "king row." You can do it if you awaken in time. And, your *time* is now.

You are the business—you are the man on

whom success depends. You can make it or break it. And, *you* don't have to break it.

Build up your organization if it needs building up by setting a standard—by leading your men—by showing them the way.

The men under you expect you to show them the way—they are going to work to the pace set by you.

They look to you to lead them.

Your business is going to be just what you make it—no bigger—no smaller than "the lengthened shadow of one man."

You must lead—so be the proper sort of a leader.

Some author has said that "life is a train of moods."

How true this is and what an important thing to watch: One morning you feel fine—you are in a mood for work. You have a cheerful word for everyone you come in contact with. What happens? Your cheerful, happy mood becomes contagious. It is passed on. Your salesmen catch it. They go out feeling fine. And they will fight to bring back the business.

You govern the results. The day is fair or cloudy, all depending on yourself.

Now let us draw the other picture.

You come down in the morning feeling grouchy. The first person you come in contact with notices it—and the word is passed along—"The boss has a grouch on." And the damage is done. The day is spoiled. The business day goes for naught.

It is easy enough to explain this. Your employees look to you as a leader. They expect you to set the standard. The average man will work hard for you, if properly encouraged.

And so, train your thoughts. Train your mind. Try to be the same each day—and—help your men.

George Stallings, Manager of the Boston Braves, won a World's Baseball Championship by proper mental methods, proper encouragement, and making his men believe in themselves and in their ability to accomplish certain things.

He kept his men on the jump.

He was the father of his team.

He encouraged them by proper leadership.

He urged them on. He told them that they could do that—or they could do this—and they surprised the world, by doing the things no one thought them capable of doing.

Have your men go out each morning with the determination that they are going to win.

Have them go out thinking success—that they are going to make the right impression—that they are going to be given the proper hearing.

Your men must be in the proper frame of mind. They must be optimistic. Have them thinking success—couple this with a complete knowledge and understanding of what they are selling and victory is theirs.

Don't give up easily.

Fight for business because it belongs to you. Fight for your rights because you are right. Bring every possible angle to bear on each prospect. Fight morning, noon and night. Fight until *you* win.

CHAPTER XXIII

PLAN AND THINK

You must meet business half-way. You must go out and find it.

You are not going to get the maximum results if you sit in your office and expect all of the business to come to you.

Remember that as each new day brings with it new desires, hope and ambition, so does each new day bring into view new automobile purchasers.

New business is created with the birth of each day and you are entitled to some of it. Go out and get it.

This is why salesmen should work the whole year. Many of them seem to think that there are certain times when it is almost impossible to interest a prospect. They are wrong. This is imagination, and, of course, they weaken themselves by thinking that way.

Just make up your mind that you are going to do business in August, December and January. And you will invariably do some.

Think in the positive, not in the negative. Positive thoughts bring results. Negative thoughts bring zero—but that's what you invited and that's what you get if you think that way.

Not only think but act. When you think the duty is only half performed. Your thinking will not do much good unless you act. When you have an idea, act on it. Do not allow it to cool, for if you do you will quite likely lose your enthusiasm and, eventually, forget it.

Be resourceful. The resourceful man will win when the man who refuses to use his brain will invariably fail.

This is one of the most important things in business life. Cultivate resourcefulness. Exercise your brain each day. The brain like any other part of your body, will waste without use.

Remember that the brain grows—the more you give it to do, the more it wants to do and the more it is able to do.

The resourceful man will do business when others complain that it is dull. The resourceful man finds a way because he believes that he can do certain things and this confidence helps him to accomplish his desires.

The man who starts out to accomplish a certain thing does it—if he makes up his mind he is going to do it.

The man who wins in business knows all about his business. And, if he doesn't happen to be the "top notcher" in his town, he patterns after the man who is. Study the most successful dealer you know.

The man who wins plans the work of the men under him—he keeps them busy—he inspires them—helps them. And the man who wins leads his men—you must set the pace.

And if you have ever noticed, you have

found that the successful man is invariably the enthusiastic man. He has enthusiasm. He has imagination. He has optimism. He has faith. And he is cheerful and happy.

The man who wins sees to it that each person entering his front door is courteously received and that he takes a good impression away with him. The more people you know, the easier it is to do business and the amount of business you do will depend on the number who have confidence in you and your organization.

Every day should see some movement toward getting some amount of new business.

That's the way to grow.

Somewhere, some place, it is waiting for you. But it remains for you to reach out for it.

And you should figure that every effort you make, even if it isn't productive immediately, is a move toward the future development of your business.

And that is the important thing to remember. Little things done each day count up in the long run.

But the thought to bear in mind is to create something each day, to add something to your total business.

And the best way to do that is to think. A little thinking will show you the way to new business.

Try it today. One thought will lead to another and before you know it, ideas will be piling on each other so fast that you will have material aplenty to work with.

You never need to be out of ideas—not if you think.

And the more you think, the easier will you find it to plan for more business.

The thinking man wins. He cannot help but win, because constant thinking helps one to reason clearly and correctly and by this method he arrives at a basis of action that will prove helpful to his business.

Emerson said "Nothing great was ever accomplished without enthusiasm."

And it is true, too. Without it we are lost and with it we can accomplish wonders, for it turns failures into successes.

Plan and Think

Couple enthusiasm with faith and persistency and no one can stop you. The enthusiastic man always lands on top.

This type of man thinks—plans—acts—he finds a way of doing things. And he is never down-hearted—he hasn't time to be, for enthusiasm keeps him up—and keeps him busy.

Has it ever occurred to you that Monday is the most important sales day of the week?

Monday should be the big day of the week, because it follows Sunday.

On Sunday, nearly every car owner is out driving and those who do not own a car are out walking.

Have you ever noticed how each one walking gazes at the cars as they whiz by? It seems a natural thing to do, too.

Those who are walking would like to be riding. And thus it is that on Sunday people long most for a car.

And so on Monday get after your prospects with determination.

You will find them in just the proper frame

of mind—some of them may have been in the parade walking.

Try it next Monday.

Get in touch with a number of the "hottest" prospects who have never owned a car and you will find that Sunday has put them in a closing mood.

CHAPTER XXIV

TODAY IS THE DAY

It has been said that it would take two hundred years to count the nerve cells in your brain.

That's how rich you are in mental capacity.

There are from 600,000,000 to 1,200,000,000 nerve cells in the brain for the generation of nerve force and the moulding, fashioning and storing up of your ideas.

Just think how rich you are!

Just think of the power within you ready to be developed if you but give your assistance—in thinking.

Suppose you had ten new ideas a day for the increase of your business. In one year you would use 3,650 nerve cells.

You still would have left, figuring on a

basis of 600,000,000 nerve cells, 599,996,350 for use—for fashioning and storing up your ideas.

This will give you some idea of what the brain is capable of doing—if you help it.

Do not forget that today is the day.

Concentrate on today—do your very best this very day.

Never mind about tomorrow, or the day after, or next week, or next month.

This is the day, the most important day of your life.

Let each day take care of itself, and as each day comes, do your utmost and you will find that at the end of each week you will have accomplished a whole lot.

The man who doesn't do anything is the man who is hoping for the tomorrows—the man who is always waiting—hoping—that something will turn up.

This sort of a man never gets anywhere because he is a dreamer—a "putter-off." He is dying mentally and doesn't know it.

And besides, the tomorrows never come.

The "tomorrows" always become the "todays."

Many a man has lost a sale because he said, "I will see my man tomorrow," or "the day after" or "next week."

Don't put off till tomorrow what you can do today.

It is dangerous practice, for you get to be a professional "hoper." And that's the beginning of the end.

Concentration and stick-to-itiveness are the vital things in business and if you would be successful, you must follow these rules.

Success depends mostly on yourself. You may be selling a splendid line of cars, but if your organization is weak, if you have inefficient salesmen, if your location is not right, if you neglect advertising and promotion work, if you are not known as a "fair and square business man," you are not going to get the maximum results. And make up your mind to it.

The great game of base ball furnishes a good text for a business talk.

The idle base ball player—the man on the side line always reminds one of the business man who is not active—who is constantly waiting for something to happen—who watches the real business man rush by him with the flush of success on his face.

Success comes to the man who meets business half-way.

You cannot win a base ball game by watching it, nor can you win business battles by sitting idly in your office and hoping for business success to come to you.

You have to go out and fight for business—because every successful business man is doing it and that is why he is a success—he fights.

To be successful, you should be planning new things all the time—new ways of securing prospects—of interesting them—of filling them with enthusiasm and bringing their interest to such a climax as will make closing a sale an easy matter.

You should plan ways of improving your service—the looks of your showroom—the work of your men—of attracting attention to your car.

Constant work means success.

The man who works is the man who wins. The victory is to the fighter—to the plodder—to the man who does not give up easily.

So do not stand on the side lines—get into the fight yourself—demand your share of the business. You have it coming to you and you can get it if you make the proper effort.

And here is the secret for success—start to work early in the day—don't wait until three o'clock in the afternoon before "warming up."

The man who accomplishes things is the man who starts out early, and as the day lengthens his enthusiasm strengthens, and when evening comes he is able to show results—for he has worked every minute and with his effort he has coupled enthusiasm—the most important assistant of all.

CHAPTER XXV

DON'TS

Don't knock your competitor's car. It's mighty poor business and it doesn't pay in the long run.

Don't misrepresent. You can tell a prospect that your car will travel thirty miles on a gallon of gasoline, but it won't take him long to find out that it can't do it.

Don't say your car is the best on earth. It probably isn't and superlatives will make your prospect antagonistic. They suggest something to be proven.

Don't argue. Your customer is always right. Agree with him. If you can't, say you believe he misunderstands, and change the subject.

Don't go into technical details unless you are sure of your ground. Most purchasers buying their first car don't know a spark plug from a tire iron—and don't want to. If a man asks questions, explain the point briefly and clearly.

Don't try to demonstrate a car without gasoline in the tank. It has been tried and can't be done.

Don't abuse your demonstrators simply because the man you work for pays for the repairs.

Don't be afraid to make calls before noon. In the morning you are fresh and so is your prospect. His mind is open—he is ready to be convinced.

Don't underrate your competitors. Study their cars and study their methods. Know their sales tactics and how best to meet them.

Don't neglect your home office. Work in harmony with it. Pay the factory a visit if you can. If you can't do that, write to them. Tell them about their competitors' methods. Tell them of your successful methods.

LaVergne, TN USA
22 July 2010
190448LV00003B/17/P